God just is

God just is

Approaches to silent worship

Curt Gardner

First published March 2012

Quaker Books, Friends House,
173 Euston Road, London NW1 2BJ

The moral rights of the author are asserted in
accordance with the Copyright, Designs and
Patents Act 1988. All rights reserved. No part of
this book may be reproduced or utilised, in any
form or by any means, electronic or mechanical,
without permission in writing from the publisher.
Reviewers may quote brief passages. Enquiries
should be addressed to the Publications Manager,
Quaker Books, Friends House, 173 Euston Road,
London NW1 2BJ.

ISBN 978 1 907123 24 5

© Curt Gardner, 2012

Book designed and typeset by Golden Cockerel
Press Ltd, London

Cover design by Michael Preston

Printed by Information Press

Set in Adobe Minion Pro 10.5/14.5

Britain Yearly Meeting is a registered charity,
number 1127633.

Britain Yearly Meeting is committed to becoming
a low-carbon, sustainable community. All our
books are printed on FSC certified paper. FSC
certified forests are managed with consideration
for people, wildlife and the environment.

www.quaker.org.uk

MIX
Paper from
responsible sources
FSC
www.fsc.org   FSC® C013262

Contents

Acknowledgements

I would like to thank Mora Brown, Gillian Allnutt, Julia Gordon, and Angela Williams for their comments; also to the Reverend Lesley Chapman, the Reverend Dr Ellen Clark-King and Nuala Furlong, who gave me advice on the spirituality of women. I am grateful to Father Kevin Daley, Father George Dolan and the Reverend Henry Morgan for their searching questions and comments. I am also grateful to my editor Peter Daniels for his vision and his help in shaping this book. However, without the patience of my wife who read my early notes to correct my English, this book would never have been published. Above all, I am indebted to a huge range of people who throughout my life have unstintingly given me their wisdom, guidance and advice.

About this book

While silent or contemplative worship is easier in the calm and regulated environment of a retreat house or monastery, it is not always easy while dealing with pressure at work or being part of a lively young family. These notes are for the beginner in silent worship as well as for those who are already experienced but have to cope with difficult conditions. The notes reflect my experience of silent worship covering a period of nearly sixty years in a Quaker meeting, twenty-five of which were as an elder, caring with others for the spiritual life of the members and attenders. What I have written is my experience with God and with the people I serve, and is not an exhaustive treatise on the subject. My aim was to write a set of notes to provide me with a reminder, during a spiritually arid time, of activities that had been of help in earlier years.

The way forward was to create an *aide memoire* and this took on a purpose that I could not resist. But where was I to begin with a poor memory for recall? As I wrote, slowly it became clear that I needed to understand what the fabric of my spiritual life consisted of, which schools of thought had influenced me, what had been my practices, attitudes and experiences. My notes of earlier years presented a problem in that they described experiences that were relevant to the time but without any indication how they had been arrived at. It was therefore necessary to re-examine activities and events of previous years and that provided many pleasant surprises when discovering forgotten occasions. Some of the memories of my spiritual journey were colourful and vibrant but others, where the path of my journey had been overgrown, led nowhere. A re-examination of some of the issues, although not always easy, and sometimes painful, was rewarding. Although the writing of *God just is* has not been easy for me, reflecting on the content as it developed has been fulfilling. The process has taken some years but there has been no feeling of urgency, only a sense of being on the right track and an inexorable need to go forward. It was a slow, difficult process but gradually landmarks surfaced, and the rest of the book came into being.

On reading a draft of these notes, some of my reviewers encouraged me to re-write the book as an autobiography, which was not my original intention, but some account of my life has been included to show something of how my spiritual journey has come about, mostly as an interlude before the chapter on "Avenues to spirituality", and another about my childhood in the war before the chapter considering "The absence of God".

It is necessary to recognise that no book can create a relationship with God. It cannot produce something that does not already exist: at best it can only help to modify our approach, and change the way we see that relationship. We all have relationships with a wide range of people, some close, and others less so, but it is the awareness of those relationships that is satisfying. This is also the case of our relationship with God. Some people are aware of their relationship with God, while others seek that awareness. For such a relationship to develop, we must decide how important it is to us and be clear what it is we are trying to worship. This means we need to understand what we are doing during worship and to discern what is likely to help us achieve an awareness of the relationship. These notes will help us in this quest; they are not an intellectual approach to worship but one for you to follow as part of a hands-on experience, and you will benefit by pausing occasionally, being sensitive to any feelings resonating within.

I have a practical approach to most things, but this does not in itself help me in achieving a sense of the presence of God. That is something for which we can search, but while practical advice can help us prepare ourselves for worship, it cannot give us that awareness. We can only wait for it to be given. Our attitude to worship and God is something that must come from within. Therefore, what follows can only point us in a particular direction. I hope that the reader will find something of benefit in these pages.

The suggestions in this book are not required all at the same time but each can be used as and when needs arise. Many books have been written on the awareness of God, and I have found them to be of great value. If you wish to examine any topic in more detail, you may like to start with the bibliography at the end of this book and then browse in an appropriate bookshop.

In the preparation of these notes I have recognised that the usage of English has changed with time, and so too have attitudes towards religion. Many people in this country no longer use traditional Christian terminology, nor do they understand the theology behind it. Using a minimal amount of Christian language will hopefully enable the reader to think around the subject of worship without slipping unquestioningly into traditional religious language and attitudes. At the same time I hope to convey some meaning of worship to readers on the periphery. The words *prayer* and *worship* are traditionally associated with vocal activities whereas in contemplative worship we focus our attention on God with silent longing. However, where necessary, the words *God, prayer* and *worship* have been retained as convenient shorthand.

While I subscribe to the non-gender description of God, I have used the words 'he' or 'him' for convenience, but I might just as easily have used 'she' or even 'it'. I have made no references to church dogma, nor do I use expressions such as "God is pleased with our efforts", "He is pleased to hear our prayers", or "He wants us to join him in heaven", as such views of God are human constructs. While it may occasionally be of help to repeat such expressions, they are of limited value in contemplative worship where the emphasis is on silent waiting with anticipation and the mind at rest.

References

All Biblical references have been taken from the Revised English Bible, Oxford University Press and Cambridge University Press, 1989.

Qf&p: References to *Quaker faith & practice: the book of Christian discipline of the Yearly Meeting of the Religious Society of Friends (Quakers) in Britain*, 1995; now in its fourth edition (2009) but the references cited here are not affected by changes in various editions.

Worship and spirituality

"Worship is the response of the human spirit to the presence of the divine and eternal, to the God who seeks us first" (*Quaker faith & practice* 2.01). It is a turning of our attention towards God, seeking a relationship with him.

The movements of the Spirit, which have brought us to the time when we want to explore that relationship, may have had their origins many years earlier. The beginnings may have been so gentle and subtle that we were not aware of them. Almost imperceptibly there can develop a desire, a restlessness, possibly a yearning for something which could not be articulated or perhaps not even identified. These feelings might be passed over through lack of nurture or opportunity, or they find fulfilment in a variety of interests and activities; or the feelings for something unknown and unknowable can grow until eventually they become identified as a desire for significance in 'the other', a super-sensible reality, seeking truth; or for some, God.

Recognising the nature of our restlessness, we seek people who understand how we feel and are able to offer answers to our questions. Some people find a spiritual home quickly, while others spend a lifetime seeking something that they have difficulty identifying. This can be a lonely, sometimes bewildering journey, but it can also open avenues of richness. Finding a spiritual home in which we are at ease is often a matter of trial and error.

Those who have grown up in a Christian environment have an existing community that provides the focus for their spiritual journey, but over time some may feel restless or dissatisfied and join the ranks of seekers whose starting point has been different. There is a large variety of Christian and non-Christian groups, and which of them we are drawn to depends on what we find satisfies and fulfils our individual needs. This depends on a unique combination of factors such as the culture in which we have grown up, where we now live, our experiences of life, our interests, our personal psychology as well as the opportunities that have come our way. We also experience spiritual fulfilment differently at various stages of life, and so what is helpful now may not be helpful later; this may eventually cause us to seek a change of spiritual ambience, and hope to find a sense of belonging in a community of like-minded people where communal worship is a regular activity. You might find a welcome sense of security in a group offering the firm guidelines of traditional teachings; or find that a group allowing more freedom will accommodate any residual restlessness from the earlier part of your journey.

WORSHIP AND PRAYER

Communal worship is the way a group of people turn their attention towards God, with a feeling of reverence and sometimes joy: in most churches it is led by a celebrant priest or minister, with prayers, readings and often lively, joyous songs; or it may be more reserved and prescribed with clear formulas of wording and strict observances; or it may take the form of Quaker worship with a silent waiting on God seeking an awareness of his will. Whether God has need of our worship is unclear, but communal worship teaches us about our faith and about some of the qualities required for a relationship with him. But the activities and tenor of the service may give one the impression of a 'God out there' with little emphasis on 'the God within': as well as a communal relationship with God, we may wish to have periods of private worship when we seek a personal relationship with him that provides additional personal fulfilment and also enriches the community.

It is easy to develop the view that to worship properly we must always be active and constantly take the initiative in approaching God, but if we meet someone important to us with whom we want a deep personal relationship, would we continually talk to them? Hopefully we would look for a two-way conversation in which we could exchange views and ask questions and listen, rather than insist on a monologue of our views and wants. If we were to meet Jesus would we insist on talking to him all the time, and only when *we* are ready, or would we also want to give him some breathing space and hear his views and feelings? If we want a more balanced communication with God it is necessary to have times when we are able to listen as well as talk, and if it is not possible to do this in communal worship then we have to do it in solitary worship.

Spoken and unspoken prayers, as well as silent listening, are means by which we attempt to deepen that relationship with God. We may feel it unlikely that God has need of our prayers, but we do have the need to make them. We are encouraged with the advice: "When you pray, go into a room by yourself, shut the door and pray to your father who is in secret" (Matthew 6:6). This private time is an opportunity not only for sharing our lives but also for waiting on God with anticipation; it is an opportunity to for a deeper awareness of his presence. I have been asked: "What is the secret of prayer?" and "Can you tell me how to pray? I have listened to this speaker and read that book but still don't have the answer." While the questioners had a hunger for God they also had the view that the goal in one's spiritual life is 'good' prayer and that this provides satisfaction and fulfilment, but the value of prayer is not in a recitation of words; it is in turning our undivided attention towards God. Prayer is a means to an end; it is only part of our response to God and has little value unless it includes turning to God in silent waiting. In private prayer the distinction between worship and prayer becomes blurred, especially if it is silent prayer. When we are waiting silently on God, the term 'silent worship' seems more appropriate.

Together with vocal communal worship, solitary silent worship can draw us into a deeper and more meaningful relationship with God. For this relationship to be successful it has to be made with complete and unreserved involvement, with no boundaries, no secrets and without any fenced off areas for which we make exceptions. We must have no illusions about our prejudices, attitudes or motivations nor have any pretence about what we believe. Uncertainties in our beliefs are best recognised with honesty rather than pretending they do not exist, or hoping that they will somehow go away. We need to be honest with ourselves and accept that any uncertainties are part of our condition at this time in our lives. If we cannot be honest with ourselves, how can we be honest with God? If we accept our uncertainties, and recognise the imperfect nature of our spiritual condition, then we are more able to accept that this too is part of our relationship with God. This total honesty with God requires us to know and understand ourselves, and also be honest and sensitive in our human relationships.

SILENT WORSHIP

There are many ways to respond to the promptings of the Spirit; in my case this has been through silent worship. For me, 'worshipping in silence' and 'silent worship' are different. Worshipping in silence is a mental movement of words, ideas and thoughts, while silent worship is a silent longing towards God with a minimal amount of mental activity. Our worship may start with words or devotional thoughts, but gradually as we leave them behind we are left with an inner stillness. Silent worship is waiting and 'listening' for God with a tranquil mind without it being busy with devotional thoughts or with our daily activities and concerns. Sometimes called contemplative worship, it is not talking *to* God or thinking *about* God but it is the expression of a silent longing or yearning. We seek not the God who is remote but the God who is here and now, not the God who is out there but the God who is also within (cf. Luke 17:21 "the kingdom of God is in the midst of you"). Silent worship requires more than just an occasional or a casual activity; it requires the complete orientation of the whole person, body, mind and spirit towards God in silent attention. It requires us to reorder our priorities and our sense of self, which may result in changes to our way of life. Silent worship is best done within a framework of a spiritual tradition that provides a structure of organised worship that gives support and the right ambience. It is not necessarily a solitary activity. A Quaker meeting for Worship takes place in silence with a number of people present and is deeper because of that.

Some people find silent worship as natural as breathing while others find it impossible. It is neither better nor worse than any other kind of worship, just different. Comparing silent worship with vocal worship is a bit like comparing two trains going to the same destination: one is packed with people singing, dancing, and praising, while the other is filled with happy, contented but silent passengers.

Those who know little about this form of worship sometimes think of it as strange and mysterious, or even do not believe it to be a form of worship. This misapprehension may be because it is not always recognised when it occurs. You may have experienced an early stage of contemplative worship during a visit to a place of worship, when you have become aware of a deep stillness, and have felt compelled to refrain from talking. Or perhaps during communal worship you may have experienced a feeling of deep reverence, or have been moved to silence that had a special quality; or you may have been praying silently, internalising the words or pondering over a devotional reading, when the stillness within made words superfluous.

At such times we are momentarily without thoughts and are sometimes permeated by a deep sense of peace. When reflecting on such occasions it becomes clear that we have been at a level of intimacy with something special. The experience may have lasted only for a few moments but we can be surprised that time lost its meaning as we were held in a moment of eternity. It is not possible to create such occasions but, given the right conditions, experiences of this kind can happen spontaneously. I hope this book will help to encourage the right conditions for you.

SPIRITUALITY

Underlying the search for God is the notion of a spiritual journey, which sometimes includes a mystical dimension of life. A physical journey has a beginning and an end; we set out for a destination and eventually we arrive. A spiritual journey has neither a beginning nor an end, and whether we are aware of it or not, it may last a lifetime. For some people this is a restless search for fulfilment, while for others it is a gradual and peaceful process, developing and maturing the relationship with their God. It is this relationship, and the awareness of the journey, that makes us what we are.

Over the last twenty to thirty years there has been a tremendous growth in interest in spirituality both inside and outside the churches. The word 'spirituality' is often used with the assumption that all present have the same understanding of its meaning. While this can create some sort of harmony, it hinders fruitful exploration of the subject. There are probably as many definitions of spirituality as people attempting to define it, many of them with strong views on the subject. Some definitions include social attitudes, some include God, and some refer to quality of life. There appears to be a consensus among those examining the subject in a systematic way that spirituality is a quality arising out of internal and external life experiences. It consists of motivating feelings and attitudes, activities and experiences so much an integral part of our lives that without realising it they are the basis of our decisions: many of us find our life experiences are directed towards some ultimate value with which we can identify. This ultimate value might be felt as a sense of truth about creation and the cosmos, ethics, relationships or creativity. It might be felt in what we experience with the senses in colour, sound, music, football or whatever. For example, a friend revealed to me that she experienced this as a strong urge to be in touch with nature and to visit a lonely crofter's cottage, smelling the peat and the heather and feeling the wind on her face.

This spiritual value can motivate us to take risks, to have a reverence for life, to seek a feeling of contentment or exhilaration: with all these variables it is clear that there is no such thing as a generic spirituality. For simplicity, the basis of this book is religious spirituality in the Christian tradition.

When we consider the experiences and motivating urges that make up our spirituality it is necessary to acknowledge our negative side, as well as the positive. Some people maintain that the definition of spirituality should consist entirely of positive aspects of our lives, but the negative side is also part of the whole person and plays its part in our spirituality. Factors such as prejudice, fear, hatred and the desire for power may all reside below the conscious level: they may play only a small part in determining the direction of some people's lives, while for others these factors are so powerful that their lives appear to be governed by them.

This is Kenneth Leech's description, in *Soul Friend*: "Spirituality and spiritual life are not religious departments or walled off areas of life. Rather they are the life of the whole person directed towards God" (p. 30). In the *Dictionary of Christian Theology* (SCM) it is referred to as "those attitudes, beliefs and practices, which animate people's lives and help them to reach out towards a super-sensible reality" (p. 549). A definition not constrained by a religious basis and therefore more encompassing could be: 'Spirituality can be defined as the effects of life experience as well as the inner dimensions of our lives that give meaning to life, and direct the involvement of our activities towards an ultimate value'. This definition can include both religious and secular spiritualities, and therefore allows discussion with those holding different understandings concerning an ultimate value, whether or not these are described in religious terms.

SPIRITUALITY OF WOMEN AND MEN

As life experiences vary between each of us, our spirituality is not only affected by our culture, families and the people we meet (or choose not to meet), by gender, class and race, but also by our psychological attributes. As life experience is often different for women and men it follows that their spirituality is also different. Traditional attitudes and structures are being challenged as women continue to claim recognition of their unique spirituality, and this will in turn affect the life experience of men and will require them to be aware of the resulting changes in their spirituality. Changing social patterns are causing traditional attitudes to be eroded, enabling more men to claim their gentler and nurturing side as part of their spirituality. While both men and women can be spontaneous and are able to laugh, sing, dance, care and share life experiences, women have traditionally been more aware of these qualities and found it easier to express them. They have also tended to be more aware of their emotions and have been willing to reveal and discuss them. Where men have tended to control or suppress their emotions, this has resulted in a different balance, with a desire to be issue-orientated and logical, expressed in an analytical rather than an emotional approach to life. In contrast to women, men have often defined their positions in a hierarchical way such as 'supervisor' and 'manager' rather that by their relationships. Men's spirituality has tended to be influenced by the need for an underlying order and stability, independence, action and sometimes aggression.

Structures in the main Christian churches tend to discriminate against women, although changes are taking place. The predominant male biblical images and male pronouns can make it difficult for some women to confirm their spiritual identity as these do not affirm that they too have been created in the image of God; nor are there many biblical references where God is said to have qualities of a womanly nature, but there are some examples:

- Being as a woman in childbirth (Isaiah 42:14)
- Remembering Israel better than a mother remembers her suckling child or the baby in her womb (Isaiah 49:15)
- Comforting Jerusalem as a mother comforts her child (Isaiah 66:13)
- Jesus uses womanly sentiments when he laments over Jerusalem (Matthew 23:37)
- In the Book of Wisdom, 'wisdom' is referred to as 'she'

To Julian of Norwich, in the thirteenth and fourteenth centuries, it was quite clear that God was not only our father but also our mother. There are many references to mother and motherhood in chapters 58–61 of her *Showings*, or *Revelations of Divine Love*: "the second Person of the Trinity is our mother in nature and in our essential creation"; "for in our mother Christ we have profit and grow"; "thus Jesus Christ ... is our true mother"; "God is our mother as truly as is our father"; "I understood three ways of seeing motherhood in God". An insight into womanly spirituality can also be found in some recent writings and poems by women (see Bibliography).

Referring to God with the personal pronoun 'she' will be helpful to some people while others do not find it easy. The pronoun 'it' is gender-neutral but many will find it unhelpful. Gender attributes are at best tendencies and generalisations, but they seem to identify some aspects of spirituality that influence women and men differently.

OUR OWN SPIRITUALITY

The value of self-knowledge during the spiritual journey cannot be overstated, as it enables us to be more confident in our relationship with God and people. Sometimes an exercise to identify and analyse the nature and extent of our own spirituality can produce surprising results, especially when we are honest and open with ourselves, and have the courage to record whatever arises in our examination.

Recognise that this exercise is for your eyes only and not for others to pass comments. It may take some courage. Whether or not the profile is reassuring depends on you, because sometimes this kind of self-examination may challenge illusions we have of ourselves. If the result is too challenging and causes anxiety it may be helpful if you are able to discuss your findings with someone who is not judgmental and who can see you from a different perspective.

An exercise of this nature is similar to journaling in which we record our thoughts, feelings and reflections for later review to gain clarity on issues. In journaling there are no rights or wrongs but we are free to express ourselves on matters which may be profound or important. The method allows us to return to previous thoughts and understand them better.

A starting point for determining your unique spirituality could be to list your activities and interests and rank them in order of importance. Balance the positive and negative aspects of your self: your likes, dislikes and fears, your negative qualities like impatience, aggression and prejudices; your positive qualities such as caring for others and generosity. Finally, add what goes to make up your faith structure. This could include what you believe as well as what you don't believe, being as honest as you can.

A measure of spirituality is part of everybody's life, and the ongoing relationship we have with those motivating factors is our 'spiritual life'. For some it is more of a conscious and powerful issue than it is for others. Because of wide variations in life experience, I have been unable to make an in-depth examination of spirituality apart from some generalities, but have attempted to provide a tentative framework for you to explore your understanding of spirituality. Spirituality includes a relationship with God, and each temperament needs an appropriate type of worship and belief structure for this relationship to be satisfactory. Vocal worship is for many people central to their spiritual life; for others silent or contemplative worship is an integral and indivisible part of their relationship with God.

Interlude 1

My adult journey

As it may help you to understand my own spirituality, I will describe some significant times in my life.

It is 3am. Time has flown and sleep is faraway. Dawn is breaking and I am tense. Not being able to contain myself any longer I leap to my feet with excitement waiving the book and shouting "Yes!, Yes!"

I had been reading *The Orthodox way* by Kallistos Ware, which is about the spirituality of the Eastern Orthodox Church, and was overjoyed to find that parts of my spiritual journey were reflected in the book. While the symbolism and practices of the Orthodox Church did not appeal to me, the knowledge that part of my lonely spiritual journey was described here gave me a feeling of tremendous joy. I grew up in the Religious Society of Friends but my life experience was such that other factors had also become valuable, and this book was just one of the many milestones on my spiritual journey.

The journey leading to that moment had been a long one, nearly fifty years. As a family we lived in Germany before and during the Second World War, and it was around the age of five that my English mother taught me the prayer "Lieber Gott, mach mich fromm, damit ich zu dir, in den Himmel komm." ("Dear God, make me holy that I can join you in heaven."). I may have learnt that prayer in a cellar in Berlin while listening fearfully to the bombs hitting our home. Perhaps I learnt the prayer in Dresden during the bombing. These were the beginning of a number of profound experiences in my life that have helped me to understand the pain some people endure and which affect their spirituality and motivation. (For my experience in wartime Germany, see Interlude 2, page 113.)

After the war, we came to England. As my mother wanted to maintain her knowledge of the German language we attended the Anglo-German Club held monthly at the Quaker meeting house in Newcastle upon Tyne. So started my association with the Religious Society of Friends that has lasted now for over sixty years.

Shortly after starting work at the age of 15, as an office boy at a large engineering company, I bought *The imitation of Christ* by Thomas à Kempis, and this proved to be a source of much reflection for some years. The translation of the four Gospels by E. V. Rieu with its interesting introduction written in a clear way and an accessible style was a profound turning point in my love and understanding of the Gospels. The writings had such an effect on me that when I remembered them at work, I would sometimes be held in a time warp of worship or spiritual reflection. This could be while I was walking between factory buildings, or watching the dangerous spectacle of flying sparks of molten iron in the foundry, or the constantly changing patterns on the pools of molten iron as they cooled. This period proved to be the start of a fusion of my professional career and my spiritual life. Whether a moment on a train, or in between business activities such as a break in a meeting or at lunchtime, my mind would often drift to silent reflection or worship. This pattern of activity was to permeate all parts of my life, whether business or otherwise.

After an engineering apprenticeship and studying for

qualifications, I was asked by my employer to work at different locations in England, then Ireland, Spain and India, helping
to build turbo generators in power stations. At the age of 28
I returned to Newcastle with my wife and the first of our four
children and was welcomed back to the Quaker meeting.
I served as an overseer, concerned with practical aspects of pas-
toral care in the meeting, and a few years later as an elder, caring
for the spiritual welfare of the meeting. That appointment was
not easy for me as the other elders were on average thirty years
older, much wiser and more experienced than I was, which
made me think there was little I could contribute; but I did learn
a lot, and was re-appointed regularly, eventually becoming the
clerk to the elders in my early fifties.

The thirty years from my late twenties were rich in spiritual
development and religious experiences. In my late twenties
I began to consider whether I had a vocation and what it might
be. I perceived no clear guidance about changing my work in
engineering, but after some time it did become obvious that my
vocation, my work for God, was to be fulfilled in the daily life of
my family and in the world around me.

The 1970s were an exciting time with a wide variety of
unsought opportunities and occasions, and stimulating to my
spiritual growth. The publication of the New English Bible
proved to be an endless source of material for extended reflection that in turn led to times of deep worship, mainly during
my lunch hour at work. The Eastern Orthodox Church made its
first impact on me with the publication of *School for prayer* by
Anthony Bloom, and my discovery of *The way of a pilgrim* and
its sequel *The pilgrim continues his way*.

Over the next years the ecumenical movement was to play

a significant role in my life. The management committee of the Northumbrian Industrial Mission, with its eleven chaplains, was looking for a Quaker representative. Since I was the only person in our meeting in industry, the job fell to me. Presenting Christianity in a modern way was important to me and the work of industrial chaplaincy was of great value, although I was disappointed that it did not include a reinterpretation of Christianity. The 1980s continued to be a time of spiritual growth. A reference to *The cloud of unknowing* set me off on a fruitful study of that classic. This was helpful as some years earlier I had discovered that the closer we get to God the less we recognise him; this I had already recognised and recorded as a condition of 'diminishing returns'. Giving talks on Quaker Spirituality to groups from other traditions required me to clarify my understanding of Quakerism. Underlying all these activities was the Quaker way of worship in a deep reflective silence.

In 1985 our local Council of Churches sent six people to East Germany for '*Einkehrtage*' (days of spiritual withdrawal), joining about seventy other Christians from the Eastern Bloc, and a few from the West, in a retreat where the cares of daily life were set aside in worship, study and developing a fellowship. I became aware of the oppression of our Eastern Bloc brothers and sisters, although they viewed this to be less of a burden than the temptations of drugs, sex and consumerism they saw us having to carry. This trip turned my attention to Eastern Europe, which had a profound effect on me. I was appointed to the East-West Committee of Quaker Peace and Service,[1] concerned with relationships with people behind the Iron Curtain; one of our remits was to assist in the preparation of a Quaker couple who were to reside in Moscow and develop relationships with the

Russian Orthodox Church – see the section on hesychasm for the effect this had on me (page 43).

Later that year I visited Istanbul and took the opportunity to visit a mosque in this colourful city. After taking off my sandals and washing, I entered the empty mosque, experiencing the stillness in the huge space. As I sat on the floor I remembered a man who had come to see me some years earlier. He was uncertain whether to become a Muslim or a Christian because of spiritual experiences he had had on his frequent visits to a mosque in Turkey; I wondered where he was now.

During a business visit to Prague, which at the time was behind the Iron Curtain, a colleague and I were strolling around the city centre in the early evening when I noticed the darkened but open doorway of a church. While I hurried inside, my colleague agreed reluctantly to wait outside and smoke his cigar. The inside was in darkness and, because there was nothing to see, I was about to hurry away when I heard voices coming from a doorway that had been hidden behind a large pillar. The brightly lit room beyond the door was empty although the voices continued from behind a curtain. I turned to hurry back to my colleague but something made me go back. With the massive walls the street noises were inaudible and now there was a stillness which held me. Slowly my anxiety concerning my colleague subsided and after a few minutes I left in a peaceful frame of mind. The transformation from anxiety to peace was so powerful that on our return to the UK I wrote these lines:

> My prayer is short and is shallow
> My thoughts are impatient and quick

The time is too short and too narrow
Lord! Give me your peace and be quick.
This place is so sacred and hallowed,
I feel it as I breathe the air;
The stillness surrounds and goes through me
As slowly I sink in this chair.
I notice the walls and the ceiling
I'm surrounded by peace and by love
I feel it as I sit alone here
Alone – except for this love.
You give me your peace and your heaven,
Your joy in my heart makes me sing,
They both work on me like a leaven:
"Oh God! I am yours now" I sing.
I walk now with peace and with stillness
Wherever my feet take me to,
The ticking of clocks have no power,
As I'm feasted with love by you.

This was in 1989. By 1988 my ecumenical activities had changed and I was appointed to the Quaker Committee on Christian Relations (QCCR),[2] a national committee that was responsible for keeping Quakers in Britain informed of the various movements towards co-operation within the Christian church, opportunities for interfaith dialogue and for responding on behalf of Friends. My nine years spent on this committee alongside thirty other people were wonderful and stimulating, and gave me opportunities to participate in a wide range of relevant discussions. This was an exciting time when new ecumenical structures were being implemented in the United

Kingdom and Ireland, and we had many discussions into the early hours of the morning.

At the 1996 meeting of the Council of Churches for Britain and Ireland at Swanwick, to which we sent representatives, the evenings were left free to allow us to attend a period of worship. The chapel was in darkness except at the far end where there were hundreds of candles illuminating a large cross. On the floor stood a picture icon and in a corner behind a screen were singers who led us in popular Taizé chants between periods of silent prayer and personal reflections, similar to my experience in East Germany some years earlier. This worshipful atmosphere lasted about two hours. The effect on me was so intense and moving that by the second night I was on my knees in prayerful tears.

While on a retreat in a Franciscan friary in Northumberland I joined my fellow retreatants for Holy Communion. When it came to the Eucharist itself I stayed in my seat, and although the presiding priest and I had discussed the Quaker attitude against the use of outward signs and sacraments, he beckoned me forward. I could not refuse the invitation and went forward with a pounding heart sure that I was not suitable to be offered such a precious gift.

This was the second time I had taken the Eucharist. The first was in East Germany in 1985 in a Methodist Church. We had come to the *Einkehrtage* to give our support to fellow Christians there. The service was nearly over; most of the congregation and the seventy participants in the *Einkehrtage* had received the bread and wine (fruit juice). I sat in the pew held back by my Quaker attitudes on outward sacraments, and my English Roman Catholic friend sat with me unable to go forward because of the teachings of the Church. The last person at the altar was about to return to his seat when my friend and I looked at each other. Without a word we stood up as one, and went forward. We could not stand aside and at the same time claim to be part of the Christian family. There was a flurry of activity as the minister looked for more bread and we savoured the few crumbs together with the dampness left on the bottom of the chalice. It was a moving and memorable occasion.

In 1989 my wife and I separated after twenty-seven years together. The resulting enforced loneliness and reduced affluence obliged me to consider my priorities and my hopes. It also made me face my weaknesses, inadequacies, fears and strengths, and the need to discover who I had become and what my spiritual assets and liabilities were. I could now throw off restrictions acquired in the past, but first I had to learn what a restriction was, and what a 'normal' personal social boundary was. First I had to free myself from the iron grip of habit before I could question aspects of my life. Friends, from widely different backgrounds, helped me through this period. Their varied lifestyles, personal values and experiences showed a bewildering range of choices that had to be carefully examined, and that enabled me to choose what suited my temperament. I was particularly helped by a group of three male friends; the biblical Job would have found them invaluable instead of the three comforters he had. Their gentleness, caring attitude and non-competitiveness helped me rebuild my life.

In 1990, while on a business trip to Moscow, I wanted to visit an Orthodox Church and after much seeking and questioning was reluctantly told where I might find an active church community. The inside of the little chapel was dark, scarcely illuminated by a bare bulb. This contrasted with the well illuminated iconostasis, or screen separating the sanctuary from the rest of the church. This was richly decorated in red and gold, with icons; in front was the priest saying the office, and in a corner behind a screen was a choir of three or four people harmonising a liturgical chant. It was February and the temperature was minus 20 degrees Celsius but the tiny church was filled with many older women dressed in black. There was a busyness among the congregation of shadowy figures moving restlessly about as they whispered prayers and bent to kiss the icons on the walls, writing notes to the priest and buying thin candles that were then lit in memory of a departed relative or friend. It took a little time to assimilate the scene and the atmosphere that was very different to my experience of meeting for worship in England. I had to remind myself that these worshippers, and this occasion, were also part of the Christian church of which I counted myself a member.

The 1990s were a time of deep spiritual growth. I was reading books by Kenneth Leech and Margaret Guenther, all of which resonated within. In terms of worshipping, I had experienced Orthodox worship in Moscow and elsewhere, Taizé based worship at Swanwick, and worship in a mosque in Istanbul; while at home alone in my flat my spiritual life was deep, with periods of silent worship lasting up to two hours, sometimes so moving that I was in tears, neither from any sadness nor for happiness; this was difficult to understand because on these occasions there were no thoughts, just an intense joy. Such moments also occurred from time to time while walking in the countryside. This was a time when a deep peace and a joy in my heart illuminated my life and my awareness of God. People sometimes talk about a sense of peace, but these moments had a depth that for me had never been there before and which only comes through worship. This joy and the undercurrent of peace have never left me.

In my fifties, around the time when I was clerk of Quaker Committee for Christian & Interfaith Relations and clerk of elders at Newcastle Meeting, a friend challenged me to be clear about my calling to serve God, which I had experienced in my twenties: without hesitation I was able to respond that it was to help others on their spiritual growth. Shortly afterwards I was quite unexpectedly put in touch with someone who had been on a SPIDIR course and wanted to do something similar in Newcastle. The SPIritual DIRection Network began in 1979 in the Southwark diocese in London, and it helps people to develop their skills in spiritual direction. She invited me to assist on the course, named *Quelle*, which lasted for over two years before she moved to a different part of the country; some years later because of the *Quelle* courses I was invited to be part of the Anglican Diocesan Spiritual Direction Network.

By the end of the decade a change was taking place in my spiritual awareness: something was missing and I was not sure what. Perhaps the change came from the Roman Catholic environment where I found myself since I had met the woman who was to become my second wife, while up to 1997 I had always been among Quakers. My wife was, and still is, a Catholic and is in tune with charismatic renewal. My silent worship with Quakers was augmented by frequent attendances at Mass and opportunities for discussions and sharing with people of a deep faith; the charismatic house worship with guitar and tambourines, the speaking in tongues, and being sprinkled with holy water extended my education with something very moving, but quite unlike my usual worship. One particular Maundy Thursday there was an Exposition of the Blessed Sacrament at our parish church. The atmosphere of silent devotion by the congregation was so tangible that it confirmed for me the importance of silent worship.

My spiritual hunger continued. The map for the next stage of my spiritual journey included: the *Spiritual letters* of Dom John Chapman, Abbot of Downside Abbey, which contains much practical advice; a developing interest in the Desert Fathers and Mothers, the monks, nuns and hermits of the third and fourth centuries; and the *Tao Te Ching*, the writings of the Chinese philosopher Lao Tzu (fifth–sixth century BCE) which contained a pervading sense of peace. Once again I felt affirmed that my journey was moving in the right direction.

Looking back over my journal notes spanning nearly forty years I have become aware of the change in my image of God from an omnipotent, interventionist, external being to something that is sensed within and is never far from my consciousness. The effect on me is a peaceful interior, a peace with humankind, a delight in the world around me, and thankfulness and surprise for the peace and beauty in my life. However, while the image has changed, my notes indicate that the tranquillity has been with me for some forty years and possibly longer. This peace has at times been accompanied by disappointments and pain, wars, abuse, intolerance and violence in society, and perhaps my condition has made me more aware of them. There have been periods of spiritual intensity and growth that have been deep and peaceful. For example, during early morning worship in the car park at work, colleagues, anxious that I might have fallen asleep, would gently knock on the window to 'wake me up'.

Avenues to spirituality

Many people have written of their search for a greater awareness of the presence of God, and there are a number of spiritual traditions and religious orders with experience and advice on silent worship, but I have restricted myself to describing those that consciously affected my spiritual life. I hope some will resonate with you and be a pointer towards your spiritual fulfilment.

These are not techniques that, once mastered, will create a relationship with God. They are avenues to spirituality that have been discovered thanks to the unique nature of the individuals or groups concerned, whose sensitivity to the guidance of the Spirit allowed them to formulate unique ways in which they related to, and in some cases are still relating to God.

With the exception of the Religious Society of Friends, these people also practised vocal communal worship. The Religious Society of Friends in Britain is unusual in holding public worship regularly in silence; it is un-programmed with only an occasional vocal contribution by the worshipper depending on the 'leadings' of the Spirit. I have not included non-Christian public worship such as Buddhist meditation, nor ad hoc Christian meditation groups such as Julian Groups of which there are between 300 and 400. Julian Groups vary in size between 6 and 15 of various denominations. Their silent contemplative worship is started by a short devotional reading.

QUAKERS

As you have read in the preceding chapter, I was introduced to the Religious Society of Friends at the age of twelve. Since then I have been introduced to other religions and Christian denominations but have never been at home so much as in Friends.

The Religious Society of Friends, also known as Quakers, came into being in the second half of the seventeenth century in England. The origin of the term Quaker is unclear but it may refer to a slight trembling of the limbs sometimes happening during ministry (see below). In the religious restlessness of that period a number of people, primarily in Yorkshire and Lancashire, came together to wait upon God and worship him in silence. One of these, George Fox, created an organisation of interconnected groups that has remained largely unchanged since then. Quakerism has spread to many countries where silent worship, without a minister or leader, is still practised. The groups practising silent worship range in size from only a few to some hundreds. To facilitate an activity of this kind, self-discipline, patience and tolerance, as well as a certain amount of gentle group discipline, are essential. In some parts of the world this has changed to meet local needs, such as a preference for hymns and pastors.

The meeting for worship

When you enter the room where a meeting for worship is to be held, you will see the chairs or benches set out in a circle or a square. There are no religious symbols, no altar, crucifix, pulpit and no stained glass windows, nothing in fact to indicate that the meeting room is a place of worship except for the deep and gentle stillness.

The meeting for worship starts when the first person enters and sits down. The participants worship in silent prayer in their own way, focusing on God and his presence in the life of the world. The silence is not just outward but is an inward silence of the heart in which all present are joined together in a deep sense of fellowship, awaiting the will of God, as each can best comprehend it.

During group worship of this nature, a subtle but powerful spiritual dimension connects each person present. As we become aware of others present sharing a common purpose, the worship takes on a deeper and stronger quality than when it is practised alone. Thomas Kelly wrote in 1938: "in the depths of common worship, it is as if we found our separate lives were all one life, within whom we live and move and have our being" (*Qf&p* 2.36). Having coped with distractions of the mind, which always arise in silent worship, we become aware of a deepening sense of peace and a certain intimacy with the Spirit. As words and images subside and distracting thoughts become silent, all we are left with is a deep stillness and awareness of the reality of God within. This form of worship underpins the whole direction of our lives, whether in business or in personal matters.

Ministry

During worship a person may feel a compulsion to relate to those present an experience which indicates the activities of the Spirit within the individual or the world. The trigger for this is not the desire to share something of interest but rather a deep urge that is difficult to resist. On occasions, this is accompanied by a slight trembling sensation and racing of the heart. Each contribution is framed in silent worship as all seek to be aware of the significance of the spoken words. This vocal ministry is supplemented by the silent, unspoken ministry of others present. While this form of corporate worship does not suit everyone, for Quakers it is very meaningful and can enable those present to discover the voice of God in the stillness of their hearts as well as in the diverse nature of their individual lives. It will be obvious that in this style of unprogrammed worship, in which each seeks the revelation of the living and active Spirit, a predetermined liturgy as such cannot be used, although the inward forms of worship can be seen by some as a liturgy (see *The Liturgies of Quakerism* by Ben Pink Dandelion).

Sacraments, symbols and priests

The Quakers' attitude to the sacraments of baptism and the Eucharist is that the whole of life is sacramental, so no part of life or any activity is more sacred than any other. They also assert that these sacraments are not essential for the working of God's grace as there are many ways in which that grace is communicated. They testify to a corporate life and experience of God that does not depend on the observance of outward ritual, as no ritual can guarantee to lead to a growth in the Spirit. Quakers do not say that to observe outward sacraments is wrong, it is just that they are, in their experience, not essential to experience God.

Religious symbols can be of great value in focusing the attention in worship. However, symbols can, in the mind of the worshipper, become of value in themselves rather than as pointers to a greater underlying truth. While symbols can help to focus our minds, their absence in Quaker worship arises from the belief that everyone has a unique impression of God; what may help one person may not be helpful to another.

Quakers affirm the ability of all to have direct access to God in both private and in public worship. In their form of worship they do not find the presence of a priest or leader helpful, and there is "no need for any specific person to be designated prophet, priest, or church leader" (Harvey Gillman in *Qf&p* 27.36). Also in *Quaker faith & practice*: "To be without an ordained clergy is not to be without either leadership or ministry. The gifts of the Spirit to us include both" (*Qf&p* 12.05).

> The priesthood of all believers is a foundation of our understanding of the church. Our own experience leads us to affirm that the church can be so ordered that the guidance of the Holy Spirit can be known and followed without the need for a separated clergy … The Spirit in which the apostles lived, … which was poured out at Pentecost on all the church, young and old, women and men, continues in our experience to empower all members of the church in a variety of ministries. (*Qf&p* 27.35)

Daily life

Quakers do not seek silence all of the time in their lives but they do prefer the silent way of worship. Nevertheless, turning attention to God and seeking the awareness of him is not restricted to meeting for worship but is for daily life as well. Activities such as having a meal, waiting for a bus, or walking down the road can all be the basis of religious awareness (the writer of Psalm 139 makes the point of the ever-present God very eloquently). Ideally, Quakers try to seek God in everything they do, just as they rely on the air they breathe and the ground they walk upon so that their whole way of life can become one of worship. This does not mean that there is no laughter, lovemaking or dancing, for these are all part of life, but it does mean that the awareness of God changes and, at its best, becomes a sacrament of life experienced in the present moment.

Business

When Quakers conduct business, they have a special meeting for worship during which the business is transacted. This is a time when the will of God is collectively sought for the business in hand. They try to leave their prejudices behind and offer their ideas to God and, if they seem right, offer them to those present. Each verbal contribution to the business in hand is framed in silent prayer. There is no debate, voting or a consensus. Eventually, when 'unity' is found, a minute is prepared in the presence of all, which, in their view, reflects the will of God.

Developing a belief

Quaker faith & practice is the handbook that reflects current Quaker attitudes to life and God, containing passages written by Quakers from the 1650s to the present day. It includes Quaker 'testimonies' to peace; equality and community; truth and integrity; simplicity; the earth and the environment, attitudes which arise from their experiences of God, worship and faith in action.

It does not however contain any statements of corporate belief or even advise what members should believe. The closest Quakers in Britain get to a statement is to refer to the 'Inner Light' and 'that of God in everyone' in our relationships with people and with God. The lack of such a statement arises from the need to be always "open to new light, from whatever source it may come" (*Advices & queries* 7). Everyone, being different in upbringing and personality, has different experiences of life, and their attitudes to God and the images of God will vary. Each will experience and understand spiritual truths differently, so every relationship with the Holy Spirit is unique. While each person seeks the will of God and the guidance of the Spirit in their daily activities as they can best perceive it, so too will they seek that guidance in developing their beliefs. The search by the individual for a belief that they can accept with sincerity and conviction can be easy for some but for others it can be a difficult and lonely journey involving much searching and sometimes pain. To impose on someone a statement of belief which *others* consider to be of value, would restrict the relationship of that person with the Spirit. Quakers, being more concerned with a living relationship with God than with intellectual theorising, find a statement of corporate belief does not come naturally to them. In addition, it is well known that as people grow older their beliefs change, so what we believed at the age of ten is not what we believe at twenty, and that will have changed again by the age of fifty. Statements of belief or creeds are only milestones that help us on our spiritual journey and it is obvious that the inscription on a milestone alters with each mile while still advising us of our destination. It is for these reasons that Quakers believe that a statement of corporate belief is neither possible nor desirable since they view Quakerism as a way of life rather than a set of beliefs locked unalterably into a statement. Although the Religious Society of Friends is inextricably rooted in Christianity, many Friends affirm that God is not restricted to Christianity but reveals himself in all religions.

Inner Light

Friends speak of the 'Inner Light' or the 'Inward Light', which is often taken to refer to God's presence within us and to a direct and personal experience of God. They are illuminated by the light of God, rather than having a light of their own within.

It may help to quote from *Quaker faith & practice*:

> By emphasising the Inner Light, we do not humanise religion too much. It is not our light – we receive it. As we are in the midst of experiences with our fellow beings, a light will come that causes those experiences to look changed. We say, in a clumsy way, that it is the Inner Light that has caused the transformation and we believe that it came from God. How do we know that we are not deceiving ourselves? In the end, we have nothing but our own experience to rely upon. In the end, even the one who accepts the most traditional religion has nothing but his own experience to rely on. (Waldo Williams, 1956, in *Qf&p* 26.64)

The Inner Light is a concept which Quakers also use to express their conscience, faith and beliefs, and because it is experiential each person has their own understanding of what it means. Friends also use this concept when they seek collective guidance from God when sharing their concerns.

Experiment with Light

An increasing number of Friends are finding the 'Experiment with Light' a real benefit. It is an organised way to bring the stillness of Quaker worship to bear on everyday issues, derived from Rex Ambler's research into the meditative worship practised by early Quakers, with the aim of experiencing 'the Light' as they understood it. There are about 100 groups in Britain, of six to twelve people who meet in an atmosphere of worship taking part in a guided meditation. They reflect in silence on issues connected with their individual lives or with the world, seeking a response. The purpose is to seek answers to difficulties in their lives and hence to know and understand themselves better. Regular participants to these meetings speak of being able to attain a sense of peace and of self-knowledge. It is suggested that the guided meditation is best practised within a group who can give support if needed.

PRACTISING THE PRESENCE OF GOD

Occasionally in meeting, I heard references to Brother Lawrence being aware of the presence of God even while he was washing dishes. I must have asked about this because an elder invited me for a meal and then presented me with a copy of the book *The practice of the presence of God*, a collection of what Brother Lawrence said and wrote on the subject of being aware of God in everyday life. This resonated strongly within me and provided a spiritual milestone.

He was born in France in 1611 and joined the army in his late teens. After being invalided out of the army, he pursued a career as a footman and later, at the age of about forty years, he became a Carmelite Brother. He worked as a cook in a monastery near Paris and during this time he counselled people and wrote them letters of advice on spiritual matters. Following his death his Abbé collated the letters together with any recollections of conversations, and this material forms the basis of what we have today: a number of translations are available.

Brother Lawrence believed that God is present at all times, and we have to train ourselves to be aware of that. In his daily activities he strove to keep his attention on God as much as he could, be it with a prayer, a glance at a crucifix or something else. He would do all his activities for the love of God, even if he were only "to pick up a piece of straw" (translation by E.M. Blaiklock, p. 21). He records that even when washing the dishes he would be aware of God. These moments of devotion increased in frequency and eventually became so continuous that they resulted in a relationship that took place in the depths of his soul. By being so connected to God, he was of the view that all his activities were, in effect, not done by him but by God, and that he had only been the physical means to an end. Having put all his confidence in God there would be occasions when he would unburden himself to God of his cares without fear of criticism. If he felt that he might have offended God in some way, he would confess. Being so comfortable in his relationship with God, he would then concern himself no more with the matter, leaving him without any sense of guilt or any anxiety about life after death.

Brother Lawrence's experience of God was so profound he was able to lapse into a silent worship where words have no place. At times, he would be aware of feelings of sweetness, delight and a deep inner peace, but he makes the point that the motivation of his activities was not those feelings but rather his love of God. He did not always find the practice of 'the presence of God' easy and on occasions, when he had difficulty with persistent distractions, he would strive to control them by turning his attention unceasingly towards God. Emptying himself of his worldly interests and attachments would help. "God is beyond understanding", he wrote, and "to be at one with him the will must be deprived of all manner of tastes and pleasures both spiritual and bodily in order that … [the will] may be able to love God" (p. 72).

JOHN OF THE CROSS

When I was on the *Quelle* course a knowledgeable person 'explained' the spirituality of John of the Cross. I was left confused, unable to understand anything. I had often wanted to know more about him, but nothing I had read made sense to me. One day while browsing in the cathedral bookshop I came across a small book which illuminated my spiritual journey: *Contemplation 2000*, a commentary on the writings of John of the Cross. The effect of this little book was electric. I was both excited and embarrassed. Excited because here at last was something that spoke to my condition; embarrassed because up to that point I had not discussed my spiritual journey with anyone, so the details were very private to me; so private in fact that I was embarrassed to read of them in the book. It was frequently necessary to close the book, sometimes after only half a page, and come back to them a couple of days later. When I had read and re-read the book, our local library obtained English and American translations of his writings that provided more spiritual food.

The approach to God by John of the Cross is also experiential, but could not be more different from Brother Lawrence. He was born in 1542 in Castile in Spain, and became a Carmelite Brother in his early twenties. His love for God and his wish for silence and solitude enabled him to find a way to God through the negation of the Self. This meant eliminating his desires, redirecting his will and feelings in such a way that they would not cause a barrier between himself and God. Then, having stripped away as much as he could of himself, he would wait in expectation that the *causes* of his desires and unhelpful attitudes would be removed by God.

John of the Cross wrote beautiful poems of his experiences that were full of joy and passion and then added commentaries to explain their meaning. The commentaries 'The ascent of Mount Carmel' and 'The dark night' explain the underlying meaning of the poem that starts "One dark night…" Both deal with the process that leads the individual through uncomfortable periods during which God appears to be completely absent: he describes this as "the dark night of the soul". In another document, 'The living flame of love', he explains how the poem of that name deals with the intimate spiritual union with God.

Careful examination of his writings indicates two stages of development: one for the 'senses' and one for the 'spirit' and each in turn has two parts: the 'active' and the 'passive'.

In the *active part of the senses* we prepare ourselves by eliminating as much as we can of attitudes and behaviour that adversely affect our relationship with God, such as a desire for possessions, seeking to be important, unhelpful acts and habits as well as pleasures we consider essential. Other desires that could be set aside are activities that leach away the time we have for seeking God. These could include seeking knowledge for its own sake (which is different to education) and crusading for a cause; knowledge is not wisdom and crusading does not bring internal peace. If we are full of our wants and desires there will be no room for God to infuse us with the awareness of his presence. It is also necessary to reduce our desires: that will diminish the power of the ego, the part of us that asserts our identity. Eliminating desires does not mean rejecting the world but rather eliminating our dependence on them, whether it is emotional, psychological or material.

When we have modified or eliminated our desires as much as we can, John states that we enter *the passive part of the senses* where we wait on God and allow him to make changes to our deep rooted attitudes over which we have little, if any, control. It is these roots that nourish our imperfections and desires, and John asserts that only God can remove them. They can include unconscious attitudes such as being judgmental, prejudiced, controlling and authoritarian or having an inordinate pride in our own abilities.

In the next stage, *the active part of the spirit*, we are encouraged to simplify our worship and move away from discursive worship to an ever-simpler form, which is eventually reduced to a single word. When even that single word is laid aside we continue to worship, not in words but in faith. At this stage the imagination, which is always active, is gradually reduced to inactivity and we then find ourselves in an uncomfortable condition. We have given up the traditional discursive worship and have not replaced it with anything similar or recognisable. The condition is uncomfortable because all the movements of the Spirit, which we once recognised as being the presence of God, are no longer there and we find ourselves at a point in our spiritual journey that is empty. John asserts that we now have to wait for God to take us further.

This is the time when *the passive part of the spirit* starts. It is here we wait for God to give us spiritual illumination as he completes the task of clearing out our *spiritual* imperfections. During the process John of the Cross describes in the commentary 'The Ascent of Mount Carmel' how he was in darkness as deep as night, and the only light leading him to God was in his heart. The light of God was so pure and intense that he was, by comparison, in darkness [3] and it is in this passive night of the Spirit that the beginning of a spiritual union takes place. We have no control over this and must wait for God to initiate it. John describes how, when drawn into this divine union, we are touched by "sweetness and delight". The feelings and closeness are so sublime that awareness of all things ceases, and cares and self are left behind.

In the poem 'The Living Flame of Love', he describes the love of God and the state of union with him, and hints "that which was once obscure and unknowing" is now giving warmth and love. He paints a vivid picture in his notes in which the soul is united with the flame of love and burns as one with it, but is not consumed by it. This means that he retains his mortal separateness but is with God in a very intimate and indescribable way. The poem indicates that the God of experience is controlling the level of intimacy with John. Contrast this with the pro-active way of worshipping with hymns, prayers and the attending theology.

The four stages of active and passive sense and spirit are not in watertight compartments. There is a lot of overlap and we find for example that while we are attending to the active part, the passive part may have already started, and we are unlikely to complete the activities on the senses before those of the spirit have started. If you wish to learn more about John of the Cross, the writings themselves are not easy to follow so it is best done with a good commentary like *Contemplation 2000*, which was my introduction to him.

HESYCHASM

My work with the East–West Committee of Quaker Peace and Service (see page 21) led me to read books on the Orthodox Church, including *The Orthodox Way* by Bishop Kallistos Ware. The book includes a description of the 'apophatic way' and confirmed to me that the nature of God cannot be understood. There was also a reference to the 'hesychastic' approach to worship which was a seed that later flowered within me. People with whom I shared my newfound knowledge were not drawn to either the apophatic way or hesychastic worship, so I continued my spiritual journey alone.

Both in communal and in private worship, the Eastern Orthodox Church is rich in symbolism, but its spirituality has a still experiential centre that is without images or discursive worship. This is known as hesychasm. The root of this word is *hesychia*, the Greek word for 'quiet', 'stillness', and 'tranquillity'; hence, a 'hesychast' is one who lives in tranquillity. It is the way of inner prayer as taught and practised in the Christian East as early as the fourth century, and it indicates a person who 'seeks the kingdom within'.

It is not divorced from the liturgical and sacramental life of the church, nor is it separated from the tradition or the atmosphere in which the worshipper finds himself. This makes it difficult to examine in depth without considering the rest of the Orthodox way. What follows here is an attempt to summarise hesychasm, without considering the effects of the other factors, as a more exhaustive study is beyond the scope of this book.

The basis of worship for a hesychast is twofold. The first is the removal of distracting factors external to the worshipper by creating a simpler lifestyle and emphasising internal stillness and peace, free from anxieties and restlessness. The second is the continuous, uninterrupted repetition of the Jesus Prayer: "Lord Jesus Christ, Son of God, have mercy on me a sinner" (following the words of the tax collector in Luke 18:13). This prayer is repeated without ceasing, whatever the activity of the worshipper. Initially it may be spoken aloud, but as the worshipper becomes more practised, it is repeated silently in the mind where it becomes a prayer of the intellect. By focusing the mind on this prayer, distracting thoughts are pushed aside and a deep calm develops within. As the prayer is repeated without any additional images or meaning, the attention is increasingly concentrated on Jesus. Gradually the prayer descends into the heart[4] where it becomes a prayer of the mind in the heart. To assist the process, the worshipper is encouraged to sit with closed eyes and to focus the attention onto the centre of the body while repeating the prayer. The combination of the prayer and this physical attitude results in an elimination of distracting mental activities, and a state of inner peace and tranquillity.

Throughout this process the mind, which is alert and centred on Jesus, links with the spiritual heart that is open towards God. Over time the prayer becomes so much part of the worshipper that he becomes as one with the prayer so that all his thinking and breathing is the prayer. Gradually the integration becomes so complete that he is indistinguishable from the prayer and effectively 'becomes' the prayer bringing him closer to God without the obstacles and barriers of words or images and without the intrusion of the self or the world. This is not a technique, but the activity of a loving and attentive heart. The whole direction of this way of worship is towards achieving unceasing prayer and hence union with God. The stories of *The way of a pilgrim* and *The pilgrim continues his way* are fascinating accounts of a person wandering around Russia searching for this unceasing prayer. The books also indicate a further stage in which the prayer becomes 'self acting', that is, without the person being conscious of praying. The simplicity of life, internal tranquillity and stillness, together with the discipline of the Jesus Prayer, combine not just to control the ego but displace it and enable the worshipper to focus his or her whole attention unhindered upon God.

The use of the apophatic way in worship also helps to bring the hesychast closer to God, by a careful examination and understanding of his or her descriptions of God: for more on this see the chapter on 'Our attitudes'.

IGNATIUS LOYOLA

Being among Catholics with my second wife gave me the opportunities to attend retreats at a Catholic seminary on Ignatian Spirituality. I had heard of them but never experienced them.

Ignatius Loyola lived in Spain in the early sixteenth century and founded the Society of Jesus (the Jesuits), a major influence in the Christian world. He had been a soldier and sustained severe injuries in a battle at Pamplona in 1521. To reduce his boredom during the prolonged convalescence he became an avid reader of whatever materials were available to him, and he found that the quality of his subsequent daydreaming varied depending on whether he was reading stories of Jesus and the saints, or dreaming about future heroic deeds as a knight and winning the favours of fine ladies. He noted that the former were more satisfying and the memories more durable, and he attempted to understand what caused the changes in his feelings. As a result he recognised a way to respond to God that proved to be the beginning of his calling to follow Jesus. He developed a series of spiritual exercises that enable others to recognise the positive and the negative sides of their spiritual lives.

There are many aspects to the *Spiritual exercises* but we will only touch on two here. First, at the end of the day we are encouraged to review what we have done during the day and consider how we responded to different situations. We start the review relaxed, open and aware of our feelings. The positive, affirming or life-giving moments are reviewed first, remembering the enjoyable feelings that accompanied them. These positive aspects indicate those things that helped us on our spiritual journey. We then consider whether these activities were good or merely masquerading as good. Were they seductive promptings leading us away from God, or were there more subtle temptations? We should also consider whether the activities were initiated by our desires and ambitions, or whether it was God drawing us closer.

Next, we try to recall the times of day that were difficult, negative or made us feel uneasy; those occasions that brought disharmony, that were life-draining or which touched a tender part within. We try to remember how we reacted: did they make us feel intolerant, resentful or insecure and how would they affect our relationship with God? We acknowledge these times too but without any excuses or self-justification.

Having noted the differences between those feelings that were life-giving and those that were life-denying, we offer our review to God in non-discursive contemplative prayer while we wait to see what surfaces in our thinking. During this silent period, we try to recognise any changes needed to our lives.

The second aspect of the *Spiritual exercises* to consider here is the exercise to reflect on the life of Jesus, using the imagination to place ourselves into the biblical scenes with him. We are encouraged to make the occasion as lifelike as possible by adding imaginary personal and physical circumstances. The purpose of the exercise is not to distort the story but to add the missing details that will help to make the scene more true to life. As an illustration of this method, read the story of the wedding at Cana (John 2:1), put the Bible to one side, sit quietly with closed eyes and recall the story. Imagine being at the wedding and identify some of the details that are missing from the narrative. Is it sunny and warm, or cloudy and cold? Is it noisy? What can you see or hear? Are people talking, singing, laughing and lively? It may be that you are just a passer-by, seeing the scene from a distance. If you are involved, what are you doing? Are you standing or sitting? How close are you to Jesus, can you see his face? Does he look at us or speak to us and do we speak to him? (This is not a checklist, merely ideas to help you think of details that enrich the story and make it more lifelike.) After a suitable period, leave the imagined scene, slowly open your eyes and recognise that you are back at home.

As in the previous exercise it is necessary to review the occasion and ask ourselves some questions. While you were at the wedding what did you experience? What did you find good and pleasant, or perhaps moving? What made you feel uncomfortable? Did you suppress your feelings, or did you laugh or cry? How do you feel about it now? What are your positive and negative feelings? What does your review tell you about Jesus and your relationship with him and God? Again, offer the reflections to God in non-discursive silent worship waiting for clarity on the changes you need to make to strengthen the positive in your spiritual life or correct the negative.

Another example that may be helpful is the story of Jesus curing the blind beggar (Mark 10:46). Having read the account, sit quietly with closed eyes imagining yourself to be there, almost feeling the heat, the wind and the ground under your feet. You might then try to imagine what the man is feeling: After many years of waiting is this the only opportunity in his life to be healed? Is he desperate? How does he feel when Jesus talks to him? How does Jesus feel? Are the people shouting and impatient or are they silent and expectant? Which character are you in this story? Do you talk to the blind man? Are you the blind beggar? Is your presence acknowledged by anyone? How do you feel? Then, as before, offer the experience to God in contemplative prayer and learn from the experience.

On a different occasion, instead of considering a new story or parable, you may prefer to return to an earlier one, to the moment in a previous imaginative reflection when you were deeply moved. The purpose is not to re-run the experience with different words or actions, but simply to recall that special moment and then wait in silence to see what arises in your mind.

There are many examples in the Gospels that can be used in this imaginative way, for example:

- The anointing of Jesus' feet (Mark 14:3)
- Jesus calming the storm (Mark 4:37)

- The Prodigal Son (Luke 15:11)
- Martha and Mary (Luke 10:38)

As well as stories involving Jesus, you can use other extracts from the Old and New Testament and afterwards recall whether you were aware of God in those situations. Then, once again, hold the contents of your review up to God and wait for the promptings of the Spirit. In these ways the exercises enable us to discern the direction of our spiritual development.

The *Spiritual exercises* are not easy to read and are therefore best used by spiritual directors and retreat organisers rather than for personal study. There are many retreats and courses available on this subject, all of which include spiritual guidance or 'direction', and even a short retreat is beneficial. The time recommended by Ignatius is thirty days, divided into four periods called 'weeks'. These are flexible periods each lasting as long as the retreatant needs. In the first 'week' you are helped to realise your lack of perfection, and in the second you deepen your awareness of Jesus' life. In 'week' three you are led to discover the possible cost of discipleship, and in the last you experience the joy of the Resurrection. A retreat of this length is not possible for everyone and fortunately there are shorter ones lasting about one week as well as introductory weekends. It is also possible to do the exercises in daily life without going on a retreat. These are called 'Nineteenth Annotation' occasions (in the terminology of the *Spiritual exercises*) and are spread out over a much longer period. If for whatever reason it is not possible to attend any one of those opportunities, then it may be helpful to make a careful study of one of the books that are available on the subject, such as Gerard W. Hughes, *God of Surprises.*

JOHN MAIN

I came across the book *Word into Silence* by John Main at a time of spiritual exploration. It lay untouched on my bookshelves for some years, until one day my spiritual hunger was so intense that I read it out of curiosity but with increasing interest. His basis is the way of the mantra, or the constant but silent repetition of a single word or sound. This too is quite different to Brother Lawrence's approach of a constant gentle and persistent turning to God in differing circumstances. This method is used by many of the world's religions, and was also known to Christianity in the first millennium when John Cassion (c.400 CE) referred to it. Over the subsequent years it fell largely into disuse until John Main, a Benedictine monk, brought it to prominence again.

John Main was born in London in 1926 into an Irish Catholic family. He studied law in Dublin, and later Chinese, and then worked as a protocol officer and translator to the Governor General of Malaya. During this time he had discussions with an Indian holy man about a way of praying without words, images or thoughts. John Main had wanted to join a monastic order for some time, so on his return to England he entered the Benedictine monastery at Ealing Abbey in 1958. About ten years later, he realised that the form of prayer that he had been discussing in Malaya was similar to the teachings of John Cassion, and that this could be enriching not only to monastic orders but also to lay people.

This way of praying, which is a form of meditation, creates stillness by harmonising the body and the mind. As it uses only one word or phrase to achieve the stillness, it is different from the use of prayer in the way that hesychasm repeats the Jesus Prayer. The constant repetition of the word spoken in the imagination leaves thoughts of the present behind, as well as any wishes and desires. The worshippers have only the mantra in their awareness, which is therefore without past or future; it is living in the now, in the present moment. This is something Jesus encouraged us to do, saying "Do not think of tomorrow, which will look after itself" (Matthew 6:34). That single word, which is supported by the worshippers' experience of praying, gives them an inner certainty that the destination of the meditation is to be close to God, the God shown us by Jesus.

John Main considers that in this form of contemplation the worshippers are not talking to God, but by being open to him they are with him, not on their terms but on God's.

This way of seeking God is simple but it requires a certain amount of discipline.

- Sit comfortably, upright and with closed eyes.
- Breathe normally, staying relaxed but alert.
- Choose any simple word of spiritual significance and then slowly and silently repeat it. John Main recommends using the Aramaic phrase 'maranatha' meaning 'Come Lord', which is mentioned in 1 Corinthians 16:22. The word is to be repeated in four equal syllables, ma-ra-na-tha.
- Listen to the imagined sound of the word, and give it full attention but do not think about its meaning.
- Do not think or imagine anything, not even spiritual matters, as any thoughts and images will distract your attention. Whenever distracting thoughts arise, do not repress them but repeat the mantra, and it will gradually overcome the distractions. This is similar to the comments by John Chapman in one of his *Spiritual letters* that in this form of prayer "You

have a general consciousness that you are expressing the want of God, or praise, or adoration, or simply the giving of self. It really doesn't matter what the words mean. It is the imagined sounds which fill the imagination" (p. 58–59) – and these 'sounds' displace any distractions.

- Always use the same word and repeat it for the duration set aside for the meditation.
- Ideally, meditate twice a day, in the morning and again in the evening for about half an hour each time.
- Meditate in the same location whenever possible.

John Main considers that this search for God requires attentiveness and receptivity. It is necessary to avoid the possibility of half consciousness or a dreamy peacefulness that leads to sleep. He reminds us of Jesus' comment to his disciples in Gethsemane: "Could none of you stay awake with me for one hour?" (Matthew 26:40–41).

This form of meditation is not easy when you first start, but with practice the mantra requires less effort and becomes less of an intruder into your consciousness. The next step is to say it without interruption in spite of any distractions, and continue even if the mantra itself seems a distraction. As you make progress, the mantra begins to sound not only in your head but also in the heart, and eventually it is not so much 'speaking' it in the mind as listening to it in the depths of our being. It is then that the mantra has ceased to be a distraction and the worshipper has passed beyond thought, beyond imagination and beyond all images, as with the effect of the constant repetition of the Jesus Prayer in the hesychastic worship of the Orthodox Church.

When Jesus advises "I tell you not to be anxious about food and drink to keep you alive and about clothes to cover your body. Surely life is more than food and the body more than clothes" (Matthew 6:25), this is not an indifference to the external aspects of our lives but an encouragement to develop an absolute trust in God. Having cleared the consciousness of thought and left behind imagination, awareness of desires, possessions and identity, while worshipping we have ceased thinking about ourselves; we have abandoned the self to God, freeing ourselves of the world and preparing to know God who is beyond all knowledge. This abandonment is an affirmation, not of the self that wants this or that, but of the self that seeks to live with God, at peace with all persons and all creation. Leaving ourselves behind like this requires courage, as we may think that we risk the apparent annihilation of the self. John Main is aware of possible anxieties, and writes in *Word into silence*: "There comes a delicate moment in our progress when we begin to understand the totality of the commitment involved in self-surrendering prayer, when we see the poverty involved in the mantra. This is a moment where the help of a teacher could be critical" (p. 23).

While the essence of this meditation is simple, the inflexibility of the prayer activity and the mechanical approach may not suit everybody. Advantages are that it provides a clear and simple discipline for daily prayer, and that it complements our traditional worship, eliminating any images of God that may be restrictive, allowing absence of thought and silencing the imagination to enable contemplative worship.

The ideas of John Main are fostered by the World Community for Christian Meditation, founded in 1991, with an

International Centre in London as well as a retreat centre, more than 250 groups across the UK and over 1000 worldwide. Much helpful material is available from the International Centre.

Our attitudes

A friend once suggested to me that to be proficient in silent worship it is only necessary to empty our minds of distracting thoughts. This is only partly true, because when we seek a relationship with God we also need to have appropriate attitudes towards him, as well as to the world. Our attitudes and outlook on life have been formed in part by our culture, our upbringing and our life experiences. Changing them to further our relationship with God may require a reordering of our priorities, our way of life and our sense of self. A difficulty for some of us is that we have such a strong view of our opinions, values and identity that this assertiveness swamps our awareness of God's presence. As a result, many of us can only think of being 'here' and God as 'out there'. Letting go of that notion is one step forward in our preparation for a closer relationship with him.

Changes are unlikely to happen overnight but will take some time, perhaps even years. This chapter is about those areas of our lives that we could look at if we want to make progress. It examines ways to control our desires and dependencies as well as reducing the assertiveness of our ego. What follows is not a set of rules but a series of options. There are no absolutes and no targets and you should pursue the subject only as far as you are able to, as there are no advantages forcing changes to a point where life and worship are not a pleasure or a joy.

SIMPLER LIFE STYLE

If we can make our lives less complicated and less demanding, it reduces the pressure to be busy, as well as bringing economic and environmental advantages. A simpler lifestyle results in an *external* peace and stillness that creates the right condition for *internal* peace and stillness. It is not so much about doing without the good things in life as about one's attitude towards living, which to some extent depends upon our personalities and the motivating factors in our spiritual lives.

It is easy to be prescriptive when we consider a simpler lifestyle, until we realise that simplicity is relative, and what is simple to one person may be complex to another. An example might be preparing a meal. Planning it, buying the ingredients and preparing the meal can be a meaningful and fulfilling activity for some, while for others it can be difficult and stressful; but given the right approach, a simple meal can be a feast which does not demand much preparation. I remember an occasion in 1985 when travelling with some friends to East Berlin. After a difficult and uncertain time with hostile East German border guards and the threat of being imprisoned, we just managed to catch the last train of the day at eleven o'clock at night. We were feeling tired, hungry and very thirsty, not having eaten for over twelve hours. One member of our group found a broken biscuit in his pocket and, after a prayer, we shared it between the four of us. It proved to be a veritable banquet as well as a deeply spiritual experience. Anthony Bloom [5] recalls in *School for prayer* a similar event when he and a friend arrived after a long journey, too late for lunch. The only food left was half a cucumber, which they shared after some prayers. He records that he ate it as one would eat sacred food "carefully, not to miss any moment of this rich delight" (p. 16). Clearly we cannot live on biscuits and cucumber, but these examples illustrate the principle of simplicity and its ability to create special moments.

Here is an example of an area where I could simplify my lifestyle. When my wife and I go out to meet friends, she dresses in a pleasing way and one that gives her satisfaction, so it is quite natural for her to expect me to dress in a pleasing way too: but that brings with it some pressures. Which trousers should I wear? Grey, brown or blue – and which shirt will match? Is it is necessary to wear a tie? Some of the existing ones may be too lively or too plain, others may be unsuitable. Then it is necessary to choose the right jacket and colour co-ordinated socks, one of which will be missing! Instead of dressing in a quiet and calm way, minimising disruption and maximising inner peace, I find complications, confusion and restlessness, and on such occasions it is not always easy to find a deep calm.

How much we tolerate depends on how important it is to simplify our lives. In *From the holy mountain*, an account of a journey from Mount Athos through the Orient to Cairo, William Dalrymple records a conversation with a Coptic monk who told him:

> I have begun to get rid of the things which clutter my cell. Just look round this room. When I am in here I think the chair is in the wrong place, I must move it. Last week I threw out my chair. I do not need it. Now I sit on the floor. Why should I bother with unnecessary furniture? Or the lamp is out of oil, I must fill it. Or that the shutter is broken and I must mend it. Why should I bother with extra food, with spare clothes, with

unnecessary furniture? All you need is a piece of bread and enough covering for the body. The less you have, the less you have to distract you from God (p. 409–10).

I am not suggesting that we should go to those lengths, but one of the targets of simple living is to reduce pressures and anxieties caused by everyday things.

When considering our lifestyle it is worth examining our interests and commitments to see whether they will take us further away from God or whether they will bring us closer to him. To say "We need to have a simpler lifestyle to be closer to God" sounds straightforward enough. We can however be faced with a 'chicken and egg' situation if we add "as we become closer to God our priorities change and as a consequence our lives become simpler". It then becomes a circular argument, and it is not obvious how to start the process: both statements are true, yet it does not really matter which statement we start from, because the process becomes self-perpetuating, and we find it is something that just happens. If our lives are full of everyday clutter there will be insufficient time, energy or space for God, so we need to reduce to a minimum those activities and thoughts that keep us busy. The more we do, the more we will find to do: resulting in an unending process that will not bring peace into our lives. If however we seek to do less, then there is less to do: and eventually we will find ourselves in a situation where nothing is left undone. All activities have to be considered, even the very small and simple ones, as these can become numerous. They are like the fine grains of sand in a sand dune that do not support our feet and prevent us from walking to the top.

If we are involved with so many facets of life that all of our thinking is filled with the noise of activities, then it is unlikely we will hear the still small voice of God. We need to manage our time and interests in a way that will remove stress and pressures; this may include the option that we withdraw partially or totally from some of our activities. John Chapman makes the point succinctly: "The more people are immersed in the business or pleasures of this world, the more the door [to God] is blocked with lumber" (*Spiritual letters*, p. 72).

Even if we have reduced our range of busyness, having the wrong kind of activity may still make us restless and unable to find stillness within. It may be difficult to make changes, but as we keep making choices towards simplicity, they gradually become part of our way of life. This does not alter our wish to go back to what we were doing, but that wish becomes less prominent in our thinking, reducing any restlessness.

A simpler lifestyle is relative: people have their own priorities as to what is important and what needs to be changed, and this can only be decided by the individual. Changes are best done gently since force is counter-productive. Once started we will find that some things become unimportant and we can then let them go. Changes will take time but they will be worthwhile if as a result we become less distracted and hence are able to focus more on God, other people and their needs. Given time, our lives and our homes will reflect our internal peace and stillness.

The media

When considering a simpler life style it is worth examining the impact of the volume and nature of information available to us from newspapers, media broadcasts and the internet. As part of our normal daily routine we require a certain amount of information to enable us to interact sensibly with our environment. Too much information not only reduces the time available for us to seek stillness but also results in restlessness and anxiety that hinders worship. Perhaps we seek too much information and need to recognise that developing a thirst for knowledge for its own sake is not only time consuming but we may find that it hinders what we are hoping to achieve on our journey to God: for example, devoting all our time to reading about prayer instead of praying.

The media can be an insidious intrusion into our lives, making distractions and demands on our time and energy. News reports are valuable and keep us informed of the world in which we live, but very often they are sensationalised in order to encourage us to return to the next news report which sometimes is padded with trivia. This, combined with news that is here today and gone tomorrow, means that we are constantly drawn into a web of irrelevant issues that do not really affect us. Television requires people to programme their lives so that they revolve around each episode, particularly domestic dramas or 'soaps' and 'reality' television, and much is invested in gaining and holding our attention. As there are also informative and entertaining aspects to the media, a careful choice is necessary if we want time to encourage inner peace and tranquillity. To leave these distractions behind and to focus on God can create a core of stability and a peace "such as the world cannot give" (John 14:27).

Seeking a simpler lifestyle also requires us to consider the restlessness our consumer society generates by making us constantly want to acquire material things. Advertising places pressure on people to want new or different products and services, whether or not they need or can afford them. The desire for acquisitions is not something new: in the New Testament we are told "Do not store up for yourselves treasures on earth…" (Matthew 6:19), and "Be on your guard against greed of any kind, for even when someone has more than enough, his possessions do not give him life" (Luke 12:15). To help us cope with the restlessness, we have to recognise what is essential to our lives, and what is not. If we have already acquired many material goods, it may be necessary to reduce or eliminate some and be content with what we have left. If we resist giving way to our desire for ownership it will help us to realise that we have all we want; that the less we desire the more we have; and in the end when we strive for nothing, we have everything.

ACCEPTING OTHERS AND OURSELVES

Making judgments is something we do all the time, such as whether or not it is safe to cross the road, or whether or not we should change jobs, but there are also qualitative opinions such as whether or not the food is too salty or the weather is cold. When we have opinions about other people it is easy to become judgmental. We may say that people are different, tall or short, fat or thin; but it is not so easy to discern at which point our perception of those qualities changes, nor at which point we think someone is 'too fat' or 'too thin', beautiful or not beautiful. Being judgmental exercises the ego by making value judgments of things that *we* consider important but they may be unimportant to other people. If the issue is not important, there is no need to make a judgment. The *Tao te ching* takes the matter further by indicating that even if we make a positive judgment we may unwittingly make a negative one: "When people see some things as beautiful, other things become ugly [by default]; when people see some things are good, other things become bad" (translation by Stephen Mitchell; verse 2). As value judgments do not bring us peace of mind or bring us closer to God, it is better to accept with equanimity all that we encounter in life, the pleasant as well as the unpleasant.

There may be occasions when we find ourselves in a position to influence the activities of others, whether in a group or a one-to-one situation. We may be tempted to guide others to conform to *our* view of the world, which can result in an involvement and often a dependency on the outcome. This is unlikely to encourage our inner stillness or peace. Our point of view may be good but is not necessarily the right one for the other person. It is better to take the role of a facilitator, since it requires detachment from issues and is therefore not quite the same as guiding others to our views. However, even facilitation can require much involvement and busyness, and this is rarely conducive to inner stillness.

When we are confronted by actions or opinions of other people we have to remind ourselves that their experiences of life, their attitudes and values may be quite unlike ours and so it is likely that their motivation will also be different. Whatever *we* think about them, *they* are doing their best and believe they are right.

> Do not allow the strength of your convictions to betray you into making statements or allegations that are unfair or untrue. Think it possible that you may be mistaken (from *Advices & queries* 17).

It is good if we can treat everyone equally, and while we need not ignore the unsuitable behaviour of others there is no reason why we should lose our equanimity.

If we want to make progress in our relationship with God, it is necessary to examine our own behaviour. Accepting our shortcomings can be more difficult than accepting other people, as our sense of self-worth makes us blind. "Why do you look at the speck of sawdust in your brother's eye, with never a thought for the plank in your own?" (Matthew 7:3). We may recognise our intolerance, our lack of diplomacy or our unwillingness to forgive and to be reconciled with others, but these, as well as smaller and more mundane imperfections, are opportunities to learn more about ourselves. Once we are able to recognise our positive and our negative attributes, we are then able to accept them with humility and consider how we can improve our relationships with others and with God. It will not bring us closer to God if we pretend to be other than what we really are, and forcing ourselves to be different is also not a good idea as it causes internal conflict; it is important to make all changes gently.

It is important to recognise what we are, try to do better and go forward but without any feeling of failure or guilt. I am not suggesting that we should be content with our weaknesses, but rather that we should not feel guilty for having them. Holding on to guilt is a feeling that will damage our relationship not only with God but also with other people. The first step towards healing comes from acknowledging the effects of our actions, and recognising what opportunities there may be for remedy. If it is not possible to clear an issue immediately, it will be necessary to offer it to God in the stillness of our worship and then live with any uncomfortable feelings without being hard on ourselves. Similarly if a memory arises which causes us to feel uncomfortable, we can recognise our feelings and offer them to God in silent worship. This done, we can then lay the matter aside because there is nothing we can do to change the past. Over time, the ability to recognise these difficulties and offer them to God will lead to positive changes within us.

DETACHMENT

Our lives always have an element of wishes, like desires for favourite foods, clothes or whatever, but sometimes a wish becomes so strong that it dominates our thinking and causes the primary focus to be on *us* rather than on God. Wanting something may be a response to a genuine need such as a drink of water, and a need is something different. It is the inordinate *desire* for something that is not good, something that is confirmed by Paul when he states that it is not money that is the root of evil but the *love* of money (1 Timothy 6:10). We have many wants and desires whether they are large or small, special or routine. Pandering to our desires for possessions, or emotional or psychological benefits, encourages our belief that our desires are important. In reality, once these have been fulfilled we are left wanting more. If we are disappointed at not satisfying them, or irritated because our regular activities have been changed, then we are controlled by them. To give way to just one desire makes it easier to succumb to the next, and the more desires we satisfy the greater the number that will take their place until eventually the process takes on a momentum of its own and restlessness fills our whole being so that we lose our desire for God.

It is impossible for both God *and* our 'wants' to fill our lives, so we find it necessary to develop strategies that reduce the potency of our desires to a level where they are either easily controlled or become so insignificant that they disappear from view. We can forcefully suppress them by sheer willpower but that is not good psychologically. It is best to become distanced by detaching ourselves gently bit by bit from the issue in front of us. If we make a list of our desires it becomes clear that some of them are more attractive than others. Whether or not they make us more self-centred and hinder our spiritual lives determines their importance. A careful examination of a 'want' may show that it is not essential to our spiritual life. Once we realise how unimportant a 'want' is, we can let it go, cease thinking about it and gradually it becomes relegated to the back of our thinking and we become detached from it; this liberates time and energy to turn our attention on God. If any attachment becomes part of our life, it reinforces our self-centredness and become a barrier between God and us. Not being held by our inordinate desires or negative emotions means we are free of their bonds. Turning to God with that freedom enables a more peaceful and tranquil interior life.

Being detached does not mean ignoring the problems of the world; neither is it apathy, which is an absence of interest and a total indifference. It means living in the world with all its vagaries, turmoil, pain and hatred, without our lives being controlled by our negative reactions. We do have feelings and emotions and sometimes these can be very strong, but detachment is about not allowing them to dominate our thinking so much that our actions are controlled by them. While we can recognise the good and not so good, we need not have strong negative emotional ties to the underlying issues. If we are unhappy at someone else's action, or an activity is 'wrong' or not to our liking then we are not free, but are held and trapped by our wants, unable to find inner peace. To illustrate the principle, if we side with one of the teams in a football match, we are attached and controlled by our desires, but the question of which team loses or wins does not determine whether it was a good game.

Detachment is responding with equanimity when a situation invites strong negative reactions, such as when faced with someone's disagreeable behaviour or lack of care: no matter whether we call our strong response righteous indignation or anger, it means we are held and controlled by others. Negative emotions can be especially difficult to control when we encounter such things as injustice, unfairness, deceit or cruelty. The burden of these emotions is exacerbated by the anger that arises every time we recall details of the incident. It is good if we can recognise and acknowledge our anger, but we will not find peace if we 'become' the anger, a condition in which nothing else matters except the anger within which seeks some kind of satisfaction. This does not mean that we ignore what is happening, but it does mean being aware of something disagreeable while not becoming emotionally dependent on it. Remember references to turning the other cheek, giving your cloak, and walking the extra mile (Matthew 5:39–41), or advice in Rudyard Kipling's poem 'If':

> If you can wait and not be tired by waiting,
> Or being lied about, don't deal in lies,
> Or being hated don't give way to hating;
>
> If you can meet with Triumph and Disaster
> And treat those two impostors just the same;

If neither foes nor loving friends can hurt you,
If all men count with you yet none too much;

Detachment does not mean ignoring things but accepting with equanimity that an issue exists and, when necessary, being willing to work for changes. There is no reason why we should not attempt to change those things that need changing. Detachment will allow us to change things without becoming emotionally dependent on the outcome, hence maintaining inner peace. Mahatma Gandhi practised detachment but worked tirelessly to free his country from British rule, not with hatred for the British but in non-violent ways with love for his country.

If we do a task because it needs doing or because we find it enjoyable, it is easy to become so attached to what we have done or created that we feel it necessary to preserve the results. We may have spent much time and effort doing the task 'correctly' while others, who have different values, may want to change what we have done. Often the greater the degree of perfection we have attempted to achieve, the less we want others to change it. If we cannot bear that others change or undo what we have done then we are not detached. In searching for perfection it is worth remembering "The sharper the knife the quicker it will blunt; the fuller the glass of water, the easier it will spill" (verse 9 of the *Tao*). Being detached does not mean that we become unfeeling, or that we cannot enjoy life, family and friends or possessions; it means not being so dependent on them that we cannot live without them or are easily hurt by them.

If we are dependent on others for approval for what we have done or what we are, it means we have given our lives to others to control. We are then attached and are therefore not free to offer our lives unfettered to God. Making comparisons and being envious of others is also attachment. If someone has something in greater measure than we do, it can lead to dissatisfaction; on the other hand if they have something in smaller measure than we do, we could find ourselves in danger of taking pride in our advantage. Competing against others also has similar dangers even when it is part of play, as it reinforces our self-centredness. Any wish for something means we are not detached; even the wish to be free from desire is like a double-edged knife. Waiting for something such as happiness, although it is a passive act, is not detachment. The only thing we should not seek detachment from is our love for God, and the love and compassion for life whether it is human, animal or nature in general.

Instead of having to detach ourselves from a situation, it is better not to become attached in the first place, by either anticipating situations we will react to, or by letting go of issues *we* think are important. This is similar to the Buddhist way of non-attachment. The moment a provocative issue arises we need to be on our guard not to become attached. There are strategies for coping, depending on the situation with which we are faced. One is to compare the situation with other major issues in life, realise that the matter is by comparison insignificant, and put the potential emotional attachment aside. Or if for example we meet apparently inconsiderate behaviour, instead of giving way to negative feelings we could allow for potential circumstances in the life of the other person that stimulated the action. Maybe it was impossible for the other person to control their actions, or perhaps they did not have the foresight that would have enabled them to anticipate the effects on others. Seeking the peace of God will prevent us fuming with anger at the incident or nursing those grievances, and help us learn not to react to those things we cannot control.

A simple way of practising detachment is to hold in our mind those issues or persons that are the cause of our concern, while we turn towards God. We do this without striving or wishing for a particular outcome, just holding on and waiting; gradually we effectively disengage ourselves from the urge to react negatively.

Detachment brings with it a release, a freedom from desires that restrict our lives, and this creates a better potential for a closer relationship with God. The sayings of Jesus, "The first shall be last and the last shall be first" (Matthew 20:16), and "Those who save their lives shall lose them and those who lose their lives for my sake shall save them" (Mark 8:35) suggest that by having strong desires to satisfy our wants we are in danger of losing our spiritual lives. The extent to which we are detached from negative feelings, but not necessarily from the issues that created them, depends on the individual. The way to internal peace is when we are not emotionally dependent on the outcome of our actions as long as our motives were good.

Like many things detachment does not come easily and needs constant practice.

HUMILITY

Humility is another important attribute that affects our relationship with God and the world. Both humility and detachment strive to displace the ego from its central position: while detachment is distancing ourselves from strong negative emotional involvement and from our desires, humility is about not being egocentric but relating to others with love and respect. Humility is not being servile, but willing to relate to others without the assertive self being dominant. The opposite of humility is pride that puts self, the ego, in central position. Pride, vanity and arrogance are the qualities that destroy our relationship with God most effectively. We are who we are, but we need to eliminate the desire to be special. We can begin reducing the assertiveness of the ego quite simply by not pushing forward *our* ideas, opinions and values. Humility is more about listening to others than insisting they listen to us; it is about acknowledging their views without necessarily agreeing with them.

We can make our contribution to a conversation without a big show and then let the matter rest; but this requires the courage to recognise that our views may not be listened to, or be ignored, even if facts indicate that we are right and others not. Our wish to be right reinforces the self, when we assert ourselves or disagree with others. So for example, even though we think that a simple lifestyle is desirable and could be helpful, expecting others to implement our own values is a manifestation of the self, that part of us that asserts our identity. This is neither humility nor detachment and is unlikely to bring a peaceful mind.

Another step towards humility is not making proclamations of our achievements or abilities. While we may have good qualities and can do many things, we can acknowledge that there are people who may be better, wiser, have qualities that we do not have, or who are closer to God. There is nothing wrong in recognising that we have skills and strengths but we should not indulge in feelings of self-satisfaction and inordinate self-esteem. A quiet confidence in our abilities is a good thing as long as it is accompanied by recognition and an acceptance of our inadequacies. We need to be careful not to take pride in our humility, and not confuse humility with false modesty.

Nor is humility self-abasement and holding negative attitudes about ourselves. Expressions such as "I am bad and worthless" or "I am a sinner and unworthy to be loved by God" are attitudes that will only undermine our confidence and self-respect. As we progress towards humility we have to be careful that our personal growth is not inhibited and that we continue to look outwards and become all that we can become.

ABANDONMENT OF SELF TO GOD

Considerations of lifestyle, detachment and humility are primarily concerned with how we relate to the world, but it is also necessary to consider how we relate to God. If we want to develop a relationship with a friend, we need to trust them and they need to trust us. In the same way, if we want an 'in-depth' relationship with God, we need to trust him. What does it mean to trust God? It does not mean expecting him to do something for us, but accepting without question what arises from our relationship, because it is right, because it seems good or because we want to do it for God. In other words entrusting ourselves to God to such an extent means we rely on him so completely that we are willing to surrender our lives to him. This abandonment is not an abstract intellectual exercise but an integral part of our experiential spiritual life and part of the ongoing relationship with him.

When doing this we take a risk, as we have to be prepared to abandon everything that we love, everything we are, everything including, if necessary, our identity. A resolve like this can be very scary and raises anxious questions. How can we be sure that we are 'safe' the closer we get to God? Can we really trust the unknown? Are we likely to be affected in some undesirable way? These questions are understandable and there are people who think, incorrectly, that abandoning our will to God is letting go of all self-control. This is so terrifying for them that they are not even willing to consider it. I have heard protestations such as "I can't take that risk because I need to care for my children, my parents; I need my job." Other responses have been "Who knows what I might be forced to do!" or "I can't let 'another' control how I behave and what I think!" By acceding to these fears we seem to want to protect our lives and our families *from* God, giving the impression that the God of love may wish to cause us harm. Do we not talk of a loving God? Consider what we mean when we pray the words "Your will be done on earth as it is…" Are they meaningless words that do not apply to us? Should they be omitted from the prayer or are the words meant to involve us in some form of participation? How is God's will done on earth if *we* do not do it? Surely we work together with God and in that sense we are partners with him. Fear has no place in such a partnership. If we stand by the words in the prayer and decide that to do God's will is important to us, how do we feel when we are faced with a situation that seems decidedly risky? Some people will be tempted to back away and find reasons for not handling such a situation, but if we are to face whatever comes our way, regardless of the conditions or consequences, we have to be able to trust God, expecting that whatever happens will be for good and not evil. Are we not told that God is love?

We do have the freedom to make a choice: either to limit the relationship with God or to abandon our lives to him. If we choose the latter we offer to give up our interests and our lives not because we have been forced to, but because we feel it is the right thing to do *if it is necessary to do so*. That does not mean that we *will* have to give everything up, just that we are willing to do so. Abandonment does not mean that we seek to evade our responsibilities for family, friends and community or deny our love for them; nor that we should not make plans for the future; nor that we give up our intellectual integrity, or knowledge of right or wrong, or our sense of the truth. It does mean being willing to set aside plans for the future, wants and desires in order to do what we perceive to be God's will; it means seeking the awareness of God with a willingness for our wants to be transcended by something that comes from him. To abandon oneself to God is attempting to do whatever we feel is right in all spheres of our lives within the context of our relationship with him. It is maintaining attentiveness to God and then doing what is necessary when the occasion requires it. This level of trust is not easy to achieve and not everyone is convinced of the need to do so.

When entering a hospital for an operation, fastening our seat belts in an aeroplane, or sitting in a dentist's chair, we put ourselves in other people's hands and trust them totally. If we can do that with people we may not know and some we may not even see, how much easier can it be with God with whom we have a loving relationship? In *When the well runs dry* Thomas Green describes the process of trusting in terms of floating, which is difficult, not

> because it demands much skill, but because it demands much letting go. The secret of floating is in learning not to do all the

things we instinctively want to do. We want to keep ourselves rigid; ready to save ourselves the moment a big wave comes along. [...] If we can persuade ourselves to put our heads back, to rest on the water as on a pillow, we don't sink; we float! (p. 143)

We can use the same attitude when considering putting our trust in God.

The act of trusting God totally or abandoning ourselves to him can for some people be the result of a sudden conversion, while for others the change is so gradual that it can take years. If our spiritual journey to date has been 'in right ordering' and not been forced, then this step will hold no fear or anxiety; others have done it before us. Abraham must have experienced similar feelings of trust when he left his homeland and took his family to an unknown destination, following the leadings of the Spirit (Genesis 12:1).

There is a big difference between making a casual decision to trust God and letting it become a way of life. It is necessary to reinforce your attitude regularly before it can become part of the very fabric of your being, playing its part in all aspects of your daily life. A starting point could be before making decisions, speaking, eating or meeting with others: you can turn your attention towards God and trust that your subsequent words and deeds will be the right ones (in the context of your relationship with him). If you do this often enough it will become second nature, without stifling your understanding of right and wrong and your ability to choose.

Once trust is total, fears and insecurities seem to disappear; we lose that sense of self as it is subsumed into the relationship where there is a total loss of ego. Once we have learnt to trust God absolutely we realise there is nothing we would rather do than set aside our will and do whatever seems right. This is a form of detachment providing a sense of inner freedom, peace and assurance. While we are still careful to ensure the safety of our children, our family and ourselves, we are also more relaxed and not so anxious. We are liberated from many of the pressures that burden us and reduce or restrict the quality of life; our view of what is possible in life becomes enlarged and is no longer circumscribed by what have been real or imaginary fears or barriers, and we are left with a greater tolerance and trust of others. Abandonment is a form of inner freedom. We are free to respond to God, free to love him.

IMAGES OR CONCEPTS OF GOD

Many of us wonder what God is like, and as there is no clear evidence we tend to imagine him as something we can understand. What we imagine him to be varies with each of us, so concepts range from a 'person' with likes and dislikes, to Paul Tillich's 'ground of our being'. We can use these images as a temporary framework in our spiritual life and focus for our worship, but it is not possible to use them as a model of God. God is beyond ideas and images and these can represent God only in a limited way.

Attempting to describe God has been with humanity ever since we became aware of powers beyond ourselves. The first time Moses met God was when God was beyond identification in a burning bush (Exodus 3:2–4). God could not be recognised by human senses, and so Moses learnt nothing about God. Years later when Moses went up Mount Sinai (Exodus 20:21)

God was there, but so very different from humans that Moses could not use his senses to comprehend him, and so the meeting took place, as it were, in a darkness. The anonymous author of *The cloud of unknowing*, written about 1370, uses the term 'darkness' when faced with God, as have many others before and since.

Around the fourth century the Church developed the concept of the Trinity consisting of the images of God the Father, God the Son and God the Holy Ghost. This is not the place to discuss the theology of the Trinity, but it may be helpful to refer to the images, which bring very wide associations, and are able to meet the needs of individual temperaments. In 'God the Son', Jesus is a very practical figure about whom we have stories and information recognisable from daily life that we can therefore understand. The image of Jesus, man and God, is in the forefront of Christian teaching and is easy to hold in our minds during worship. 'God the Father' however is not so clearly definable, and so we find it necessary to draw on our experience of life for an understanding of a fatherly figure. For those who have had unhappy experiences with fathers or other men, the image of 'God the Father' may be unhelpful and have a negative effect on their relationship with God, so that the image of God with womanly qualities may be preferred. 'God the Holy Spirit' has no bodily form, is impossible to visualise, and therefore does not lend itself to imagery as easily as the other two. There are however many people who find 'the Holy Spirit' or simply 'the Spirit' the most meaningful concept and prefer it. Some people find it helpful to imagine God as being internal to them, while others find it easier for him to be external. This visualisation is not essential, as God is both, as well as neither, he just is. If there is a need for a preference then stay with what you have, until it is no longer needed.

We may have been given an impression of God when we were young that was intended to be a helpful introduction to our faith structure, but as the years passed and our spiritual journey continued, it will have changed to something that more accurately reflects our experience of God and of life. We have developed an impression of him in words and attributes we can understand. We can do no other. However, this restricts our view of God to human concepts and therefore reduces the *unidentifiable* God to a set of values arising from our own imagination and psychology. This means he is no longer that transcendent super-sensible reality but merely an invisible something that is a bit like us. In other words, he is no longer God.

We have to beware of giving God human attributes because these freeze the development of our relationship with him, and we then think of him only with human qualities. We can become so attached to our feelings *about* God that eventually we will equate them *with* God. For example, in our deepest and most intense moments of worship we can be aware of a deep sense of peace and love and therefore assume that God *is* love. If we agree that God is beyond human understanding, it may be difficult to justify the description that he *is* love even though we are aware of him through the *medium* of love. As love is something we can understand, experience and hold onto, it is appropriate for us to use that image, as long as we understand that the image is only our impression.

The image of 'light' is used in the fourth Gospel; it is also used by Quakers and the Eastern Orthodox Church. These images are valid for many people but others find their own words to use that remind them of God. A friend revealed to me: "As a child I saw God as having the qualities similar to those of a great big golden retriever – always welcoming and an image of unqualified love, kindness and gentleness! After sixty years I still find it a good image." Whatever image we use, we experience God but not with our senses of seeing, touch, or smell: rather, inside ourselves where we know him "beyond knowing".[6] It is a direct personal experience of his presence beyond what we have studied and learnt, and such an internal experience makes a description of what he is like impossible.

As we each have our own personal concepts of God, we may well find that these change during the course of our spiritual journeys. There are times in our lives when another impression of God is easier to understand or more meaningful, and at such times it may be appropriate to change it, but this needs consideration, and not abandoning one concept for another because it is fashionable. Instead of developing a relationship with God that is uniquely real and meaningful for us, to follow the latest ideas unthinkingly is like a rabbit bolting out of the security of its burrow into the open, only to sit terrified and immobilised not sure which way to run; it could even be to exchange one prison for another. Sometimes the only way we can make sense of our perception of God in the world is to hold different and possibly conflicting views of him simultaneously and then use each when it appears to be appropriate and credible. This does not make us dishonest but on occasions it is the only way we can make sense of our faith structure and the world around us. There may be people who find our inconsistency difficult to cope with but that is something we have to accept.

THE APOPHATIC APPROACH

We learn from the stories of Moses and the author of *The cloud of unknowing* that the closer we get to God the more we realise how little, if anything, we know of him, so we have to beware of people or groups who claim certainty of knowledge about the nature of God. Among many who have written of the inability to describe God, Gregory of Nyssa (c.335–c.395 CE) wrote in his life of Moses:

> This is the seeing that consists in not seeing, because that which is sought [i.e. God] transcends all knowledge being separated on all sides by incomprehensibility as [if] by a kind of Darkness'. (*Life of Moses* 2.163, in *Light from Light* p. 49)

It may be helpful to explore this idea further. We recognise all of the positive descriptions of God as light, love, spirit or mother, but while he is all of these, he is also none of them, as he is much more. In an attempt to cope with this we can add a negative qualification to our positive statement and so recognise that he is not simply the positive description, he is more.

This is the apophatic, or negative, approach. It is an attempt to look beyond a description of God and therefore reduce speculation about his nature. The apophatic qualification negates the positive or cataphatic description of God and is a way to help worshippers recognise their inability to describe God. Thus we could say: "God is love but he is not love because he is beyond love; he is greater than love." This does not belittle God's love for us or our love for him, but is an attempt to overcome any restrictions arising from our attempt to describe the nature of God.

We may get a better understanding of the apophatic way from other examples:

'God is light but he is not light because he is greater than light.'

Similarly but with a slightly different perspective:

'God is beyond light but he is also beyond darkness.'
'God is not anything he is said to be.'
'God is life but he is not life, he is beyond life.'

All this results in a freedom that is unrestricted by human concepts. It allows us to reach towards God, unfettered by imagining him to be something in particular. It allows us to reach out to God who is greater than our words. Then, going beyond positive and negative words by leaving them behind, the apophatic way moves beyond affirmation and negation to a 'negation of knowing', when we realise that we do not know God and cannot use words to describe him. Eventually a position is reached when this negation of knowing becomes one of a number of factors that create a condition that may eventually lead to spiritual union. Many mystics in history have used the apophatic way including Meister Eckhart, John of the Cross and the author of *The cloud of unknowing*. Here are some examples of cataphatic and apophatic assertions about God taken from *The Orthodox way* by Bishop Kallistos Ware.

All that we affirm concerning God, however correct, falls far short of the living truth […] Having made an assertion about God, we must pass beyond it: the statement is not untrue yet neither it nor any other form of words can contain the fullness of the transcendent God […] The way of affirmation must be balanced by the way of negation. [...] Destructive in outward form the apophatic approach is affirmative in its final effect. [...] Our negations are in effect a super-affirmation (p. 16–17).

God is present not merely [...] as a nameless force, but in a personal way. God who is comprehensible, is not God (p. 13).

God is both further from us and nearer to us than anything else. [...] We find God grows evermore distant and evermore intimate, well known yet unknown. [...] God is both 'end point' and 'starting point' [...] he is the host who welcomes us at the conclusion of the journey, yet he is also the companion who walks by our side every step upon the Way. [...] he is both the inn at which we rest for the night and the final end of our journey (p. 14).

If we say that he is good or just we must at once add that his goodness or justice is not to be measured by our human standards. [...] If we say that he exists, we must qualify this immediately by adding that he is not [...] an existing object among many (p. 16).

The thick darkness into which we enter with Moses turns out to be a luminous dazzling darkness (p. 17).

When handled correctly, apophatic theology can be an asset to our spiritual lives, but it is necessary to ensure that when considering a negative proposition, a positive one always accompanies it. If the focus is solely on the negative, we may find ourselves questioning the existence of God, and *in extremis* conclude that there is no God. (See "The Absence of God", page 119).

SUMMARY

This chapter has been about losing the restless assertiveness of our identity that says "This is me" and "I am…", those things that we emphasise because we want to be noticed. While they rightly identify our uniqueness and our places in relationships and the world, an overemphasis on them makes us increasingly self-centred. It is necessary to recognise this danger when we are trying to create a focus on God. Which of the approaches described above is most helpful depends on the individual. Simplicity of living removes the distracting clutter of life; detachment helps us face difficulties without being oppressed by them; humility enables us to meet the world as equals but with gentleness and without strife; and abandonment brings trust in God in the present moment.

These attitudes and approaches to God, together with a loss of internal images, create an inner peace that enables us to reach out more easily to the God who just is. They help us to lose much baggage, resulting in a sense of freedom that brings a lightness of heart, a longing for God, a joy and peace that transcends all. The release from one's anxieties, and not holding onto the old values of self, bring opportunities for spiritual growth. Later in our lives, with the value of hindsight, we realise that our feeling of freedom has evolved from these attitudes. As our relationship with God deepens and becomes all embracing, our attitude to life changes, priorities change and some things that were once important become less so.

Each of us needs to decide how far we want to go. This chapter has been intended only to give some idea of what can be sought; some suggestions may appear extreme, and further than some people wish to go, but they are principles to which people are drawn, some more so than others. They are not essential to a relationship with God, but each brings with it some value that deepens it. We should not force change on ourselves, but rather allow it to come naturally from our experience of God and from our resulting reflections. It is necessary to be gentle with ourselves and proceed only if it feels right. As struggling is counter-productive we should simply be what we are and remain still. We should continue to live life and enjoy it, allowing changes to happen naturally without force, and then the rest will follow.

Daily activities

PRACTICAL MATTERS

If you are new to silent worship it is difficult to engage in it for a long period. This chapter consists of short daily activities that will help to orientate your focus onto God. They are short moments of worship that also prepare you for longer periods.

God is everywhere but also nowhere, he just is, and our awareness of him is an obscure but very real feeling we experience in our subjective lives. Whether we are praying, riding a camel, parachuting or simply preparing a meal, God cannot help but be with us, here and now: it is only our awareness of him that is elusive. This awareness is not attainable in some mechanical way like unlocking a door, but is something internal that grows during our spiritual journey. There is nothing we can do to overcome that other than to orientate our attention and then to wait in stillness and with patience.

To practise turning our attention frequently towards God so that it becomes a core part of our way of life, the way we think and do things, is the way forward. How much time and effort we devote to that depends on our circumstances and inclination. Finding opportunities to turn to him is sometimes a challenge but with a bit of careful thought we can succeed. We can reach out to God in small ways for short periods: ideal opportunities are when our work is of a simple routine nature that does not require much concentration. Washing dishes, cooking, picking berries or walking are examples that can be undertaken with that focus. In those conditions, our attention on God co-exists with our actions. These moments can include spoken or unspoken prayers or other meaningful words. A collection of our favourite prayers, psalms, readings or hymns (either written or, better, remembered) can be helpful at these times. Frequent practice using short phrases or single words can cause them to surge into our consciousness involuntarily at unexpected moments, sometimes with a spontaneous vocal expression reminding us of this dimension of life. When we are more experienced, our activities are done with the quiet knowledge that we are close to God at the same time. It is on these occasions that work and worship are intertwined in such an intimate way that our work is part of worship.

If our everyday activities are more stressful, requiring much mental participation, it is difficult if not impossible to find internal calm and stillness. It is then necessary to have a strategy to slow our activities down so that they are temporarily on hold. A spinning cartwheel or bicycle wheel is a good analogy. As the rim is moving quickly we cannot follow the progress of individual spokes, but as our eyes move towards the centre of the wheel, the circular movements becomes slower and eventually we arrive at the centre where there is no movement, just stillness. Similarly as we temporarily move away from the busyness of our daily lives and the stimuli that accompany them, we can find that still centre within.

It is sometimes useful to have a simple mechanism to act as a reminder to slow down. These reminders help to create opportunities for a brief focusing of attention on God in whatever way might be appropriate. For these occasions a kitchen timer, a mobile phone, a digital watch or even a computer can be used.

If an occasion is not opportune then let it pass, continue to work without feeling guilty and look forward to the next opportunity. Some people find it relatively easy to turn to God, while others find it difficult: if you belong to the latter group you should not be disheartened because every attempt to focus your attention on God strengthens your ability and furthers your relationship with him.

Time and circumstances permitting, these moments of devotion can be extended. Half an hour every morning is good, and if you feel the need and opportunities arise, it can be increased with a second occasion later in the day. Before breakfast is helpful, while the issues of the day have not yet claimed your attention and stimulated the mind; those who are not morning people may prefer to start later, but opening the post or the diary and listening to the news are all opportunities for a myriad of activities to descend like insects feeding in a field of wild flowers – all is relatively peaceful until you walk through the field and then they swarm around you.

Evenings can be good for some people because the busyness of the day has subsided. There is the risk of sleepiness, but it is possible to overcome this by doing a few gentle yoga exercises. Not only do they stimulate, so that you become more alert, but if done with your focus on God they are also a good preparation for worship. If you do fall asleep because of tiredness you should not be unduly concerned as it is obviously what the body needs at that moment, although if you fall asleep regularly it will be necessary to examine your lifestyle.

Just as you cannot breathe slowly after running for a bus, you cannot easily enter silent worship if your mind is being held by your interests. For a period of worship it is desirable to have a still mind that is not racing or preoccupied with daily activities. Stilling the mind is not the same as inner stillness. Stilling the mind reduces the restlessness of thinking and activities temporarily, whereas inner stillness is a more permanent tranquillity. There are many factors contributing to inner stillness but reducing mental activities is a prerequisite. Instead of trying to deal with restlessness or pressure once it is established, it is better to prevent it happening in the first place: but that may not be easy, as it depends on your lifestyle. It can be helpful to avoid situations such as:

- Frequently checking the time to see if the bus is late or whether you will be late at your rendezvous.
- Rushing for an appointment and fretting about the possible consequences of being late.
- Being outraged or angry at a disagreeable incident.
- Rushing to clear jobs and chores as quickly as possible in order to gain a few extra minutes of worship.
- Rushing from one place to another, when walking peacefully will suffice.
- Being preoccupied with something else.
- Always being busy with no time for yourself.

Before starting a task, instead of rushing to achieve a difficult deadline, assess the time available then offer the task to God and proceed steadily until it is necessary to stop. If the work is incomplete by the end of the time available, if you can, let it rest and stand back in the peace that comes from God and worry no more.

When trying to cope with a number of things at the same

time, one way of slowing down is to focus only on the current activity and with deliberation ignore the remorseless pressure from all the issues clamouring for attention. It may be better on some occasions not to start the work in the first place. The path to stillness is to handle only one task at a time. Some people claim to be capable of multi-tasking, but it is important to let each task have its own time and place. This attitude of mind may not be easy to achieve or to maintain in today's competitive world, especially when we are required to do additional tasks in order to improve productivity. However, with a little thought we can find other examples where we can prevent tension or pressure developing.

As part of our daily activities we also need to create time for some devotional *reading, reflection and meditation*. These are part of spiritual life as they broaden our horizons, helping us understand ourselves and examining our relationship with God. They can also generate feelings of peace and tranquillity that enable us to slip into periods of spontaneous silent worship.

When *reading* a piece of devotional literature, a sentence, word or a phrase may stand out as being particularly meaningful and resonate within. When that happens, stay with the meaning of the words and allow the mind to be still. As you wait for illumination, respond not in a way you think would be appropriate, but in the way you feel internally moved to do. This way you will receive spiritual nourishment. If nothing holds your attention and the words appear to be bland and uninteresting, try a different paragraph. However, resist the temptation to skip from paragraph to paragraph until the end of the chapter or book has been reached and restlessness has developed, as that is not worship; try to stick to a maximum of two to three paragraphs and revisit them again and again. You can also reflect on individual words or phrases, asking yourself what the writer intended to convey by them, with a view to discerning their fullest meaning.

Recognising that spirituality is worldwide and finds expression in other cultures, we should not restrict ourselves to literature arising primarily from our own tradition. With time, we will be able to discern what may be conducive to creating internal stillness or furthering our spiritual journeys.

Reflecting on your spiritual life can be of value as it provides understanding as well as a sense of direction. It can be a good preparation for worship to think about your spiritual life and its content, where you have been and where you appear to be going, and your relationship with God, as well as to reflect upon occasions when the workings of the Spirit have become visible. During worship itself you need to lay such reminders aside, while not denying those things that have brought you to this point in your journey.

Meditation describes a range of activities: it may be based on an activity such as breathing or walking, or it can consist of the constant silent repetition of a single word or a rhythmic phrase, the effect of which is to stop your wandering thoughts and ensure that your whole awareness is only the sound or meaning of that word. For some people meditation is an end in itself, but for many it is a means of clearing the mind of distracting thoughts as a preparation for worship. For others it can be a form of contemplative worship.

THE SACRAMENT OF THE PRESENT MOMENT

I realised recently that there seems to be a natural tendency in me to seek the awareness of the present moment. I remember quite clearly at the age of six regularly sitting in the early morning sun savouring the silence of the countryside and the warmth of the sun. In my thirties, on my way to or from work I would stop my bicycle on a quiet part of the countryside and simply be aware of the quiet, the clouds, the mist or the sunshine without thought. Later, in my fifties, I valued the peaceful midday riverside outside Newcastle upon Tyne, and would enjoy it in a worshipping attitude. Sometimes there would be moments of emptiness yet at the same time fullness, occasions when everything stood still. I am never quite sure if these are moments of worship or simply moments of wonder; perhaps they are both.

Awareness of the present moment is a valuable component of the spiritual life because not only can it help to still the mind, but it is also of great assistance in worship. When turning our focus to the present moment we can recognise that a certain amount of planning for the future is desirable. However, if we spend all our time thinking and worrying about the future not only will it make us restless – and perhaps anxious and unhappy – but we will also miss the opportunities of the present, of the now. We cannot ignore the past: we have to live with the consequences and recognise that they cannot be altered, so all we can do is accept what has been. We can cherish the good and cope as best as we can with the uncomfortable memories that are sometimes stimulated. It is also necessary to recognise that deliberately reliving difficult memories does not bring peacefulness.

It is only in the present moment that we can experience or do anything. It is only in the present that we breathe, laugh, cry and relate to others. If we say, "I want to be happy," then when can we be happy? Yesterday? Tomorrow? Will we be here tomorrow? The only real time is now. To be aware of the present moment is deceptively simple in concept but it must be practised if it is to be of value. There are two options.

The first, at its simplest, is to be aware of what you are doing at any given moment to the exclusion of any other mental activity. So for example, when someone says, "Isn't it a lovely day", then for that *instant* the mind is aware only of the beauty of the day to the exclusion of all other activity whether mentally or physically. When eating an orange, you can be aware of eating the first segment completely before turning your attention to preparing the next segment. You can also be aware of the present moment in a variety of other ways: by giving yourself a few moments before or during a meal. You can focus solely on the food in the mouth and swallow it without being distracted by other activities around you, and before preparing the next mouthful. A simple example is to eat one grape. Hold it in the palm of your hand; look at it; note the texture, the colour, the aroma. There is nothing else in your thinking – nothing in the whole world. Now place it in the mouth, feel the texture taste the flavour; now swallow. It is only now that you pick up the next grape and repeat the procedure. Similarly when meeting another person you can be aware of their presence to the exclusion of everything else around you. Waiting for a bus, watching a sunset or listening to a moving piece of music can be other opportunities to focus on the present moment. Being alive only to the present moment has the effect of excluding, for that moment, the interruptions and the clamour of daily life.

In the second option the awareness of the present moment can be refined further. If you focus on what you are doing, the 'I' in "I am sitting" or "I am walking" disappears, and the activity becomes simply sitting or walking. Gradually this too goes and you find yourself at the point when you 'just are', simply being in a situation but without thoughts. This type of focusing brings the body, the mind and the surroundings into harmony, ensuring you are not doing one thing while the mind is preoccupied with something else. There is no intellectual effort here.

For some people awareness of the present moment is an end in itself, but here the attention is on the value it can bring to worship when it can become sacramental. These are times when, without our realising it, and without any effort on our part, the present moment just is. They are not moments of intellectual activity but of feeling, and the more focused we are the more profound is that sense of the present moment. This is a time when awareness of the present moment envelops our whole being and changes in nature to become worship.

For example when communicants receive the bread and wine during the Eucharist, there is nothing in their awareness except the present moment in devotion. I have experienced this when worshippers went forward to receive the bread and wine, and the quiet prayerful sounds arising from the congregation created an ambience that drew me into a spiritual participation of that sacrament, without my ever having left my seat.

A number of other occasions come to mind that have been significant for me. During a Sunday morning service, we had come to the moment when the Creed was being said; I closed my eyes and without recognising the words, heard the devout murmur of the two hundred and fifty worshippers around me. The atmosphere of devotion was very tangible as I became part of the Creed itself.

On another occasion, I was present during charismatic worship. The singing was lively, the guitarist was inspired, the tambourines were beating out the rhythm and there was joy all around. I felt the power of the worship drawing me even though it was quite different from the style I was accustomed to. Being unsure how best to participate I sat on the floor, closed my eyes and let myself sink into the devotional atmosphere around me. The quality of the occasion became so sacred that I felt an absorbing sense of the presence of the Spirit that held me in a deep peace. The group and I were in unity but worshipping in our own ways; they had an uplifting sense of joy and praise while I experienced a profound stillness and a deep peace in the midst of the singing and music.

Once, during a period of silent worship in solitude in a cornfield, I became aware of the warmth of the sun, of the birds and insects. Beetles and spiders crawled over my hands and feet and a wren was foraging noisily on the nearby wall. Their presence did not disturb me – rather it was as if they were part of me and I was part of them. I became aware of my relationship with everything around me: the corn, the creatures and all the inanimate matter; I was a homogeneous part of the whole of creation and had no separate identity, only a deep sense of peace and wholeness.

After such occasions we are aware of having been close to God. The feelings of deep peace remain with us for a long time, but the hope to return to that condition lasts forever. If we accept the premise that worship is our response to God seeking us, then these moments are pure worship, occasions when we engage with God. The awareness of the present moment is something to seek not only during worship but also at any time of the day. When this is done with the perception of God's presence it can be a powerful spiritual experience, a sacramental moment.

Preparation for worship

All the activities described in the previous chapter, if done with our attention on God, are worship. For periods longer than a few minutes, a certain amount of preparation will be helpful. Any form of worship, whether vocal or silent, is enhanced by the preparation of heart and mind as this enables the time to be more valuable. How helpful the preparation is depends on how well we do it, on our preferences and our needs.

At its simplest, preparation can include anticipating the occasion with pleasure; thinking about the approaching period of worship while positioning a chair or selecting a devotional book. If you are at home, a short piece of quiet music or a lighted candle may help focus your anticipation. The presence of an icon or a cross can also be helpful for some people. Any part of the day can be used for worship as long as it is not immediately after a meal, when you may feel drowsy, and for the same reason it is useful to find a location that is cooler rather than very warm. Depending on what you are doing, a good location might be a car in a quiet car park, a church, or a corner at home.

Avoid places that may have claims on your attention such as the garden, a cluttered desk or a kitchen, and busy areas at your workplace. External peace and stillness assist in creating internal peace so it is helpful to seek a quiet location. Wherever you seek to worship it is unlikely that external noises will be entirely absent. Those who seek total silence do not always find it easy living in an active world because the more silence they seek, the more noise they find. Even in the hills or in the desert there are sounds made by insects or the wind. Finding a place to worship that is devoid of noise is difficult if not impossible, so we have to make the best of what is available and manage any intrusions. If a quiet place is not available, steady noises such as rain, wind in the trees or distant traffic are easier to accommodate than loud intermittent noises. As we are programmed to identify, analyse and respond to the spoken word it is best to avoid places where there is talking or a radio playing.

Many people are so used to noise that it becomes difficult for them to function without background noise from radio, television, or recorded music. If you are not used to being alone with your thoughts, and need the company of sounds, you will have to face this difficulty when you seek silent worship. In silent worship there is only us and a silent God, and filling our minds with the sounds leaves no space for God. Being aware of intrusive sounds makes it impossible to give him our undivided attention.

While we can close our eyes to exclude our surroundings, we cannot close ourselves off from the awareness of sounds and it will be helpful to develop strategies for coping with them. A fundamental requirement is not to be irritated by intrusive sounds as this prevents internal peace and stillness. One way of dealing with it is to accept the inevitability of the presence of the noise, recognise that you do not require it, and then gently lay it aside.

Another way is to allow the sounds to recede slowly into the background of your awareness as you focus the attention on sounds nearer to you. These in turn will recede as you become aware of sounds even closer, such as your breathing or even the blood coursing through your veins. By moving the focus of your listening ever inwards, the external sounds gradually dissolve further into the background where they become no more than a quiet murmur. With regular practice the distant sounds of the world going about its business will no longer disturb. This ability has to be practised regularly or it will fade away. In the early stages of silent worship, most of us require external solitude and silence; when we are more experienced we can worship anywhere given reasonable conditions, and these requirements while still very desirable become less essential. It is important not to feel resentful about intrusive noises and just accept them as part of everyday life. Eventually you will be able to incorporate them into your silence, and then let them fade into the distance.

When you have found a place that is the best you can hope for in the circumstances, try to avoid any physical discomfort, no matter how slight, as this will take your attention and therefore interrupt your worship. Whenever possible, try anticipating areas of potential discomfort and minimise them. Clothing should be loose, comfortable and provide warmth. The sitting position should be reasonably upright on the floor or on a comfortable chair, but not a deep armchair since this can be too relaxing. If sitting in a chair, do not cross legs at the knees as it may be necessary to uncross them later and so disturb your stillness; cross them at the ankles or not at all. Place the hands where they rest comfortably but without intertwining fingers.

Relax tense muscles, so they do not intrude. Start at the top of the body by relaxing the frown on the forehead and then the smiling muscles around the mouth and the eyes. Ignore distractions such as a tickle on the face or an itchy nose as these will cease on their own. Then, having felt the weight of the body on the chair, feel the weight of the shoulders and arms, and allow the breathing to slow down naturally. Gradually you become unaware of your body, but the mind remains sharp and you are aware only of the rhythm of your breathing.

If you are restless or the mind is racing, the preparations above and in the "Practical matters" section may not be adequate. You can focus your attention by engaging the mind in a non-discursive activity that has a calming effect. This is not the same as recognising 'the present moment', which focuses on what is happening around us at any one time.

One way to slow down a busy mind is to be aware of your breathing to the exclusion of anything else around you. Focusing on the breath excludes the external world by eliminating discursive thoughts and helps to still the mind. To start, focus the attention on each outgoing breath as it passes the tip of the nose. Feel each invisible movement of air and silently count each breath. When a count of five has been reached, start the count again. This limitation is necessary because counting to higher numbers results in a focus on the number itself, and this will in its turn become a distraction. Gradually, as the breathing slows down it becomes shallower and eventually is hardly noticeable. An alternative to counting which may be better is to repeat, in the mind, a single syllable word of a spiritual nature with each outgoing breath. As you continue using the same word you are gradually left with a mind that has ceased racing and is focused on God. As even these words become intrusive you leave them behind, enabling you to reach a centre of deep peace and stillness where thoughts have no place.

A different breathing meditation is to imagine the journey of the movement of air as if it were travelling through your body. Starting with closed eyes, be aware of the movement of air as it passes the tip of the nose, as described above. After a short time, focus on the feeling of the air passing the back of the throat. Next, recognise a slight movement of the chest as the breath moves into the lungs. As your attention moves further down the body you become aware of a small movement of the waist as if the next few breaths had descended further down. As the imagined journey of more breaths moves further down to your seat, you are no longer conscious of the body or any movement. The awareness of the breathing disappears, your mind too has ceased moving, and you are at peace seeking God in worship. Remain at each of these stages for a number of breaths before going onto the next. This process stills the mind by clearing out the clamour of your thoughts enabling you to turn to God. Adding a simple word with each outgoing breath such as 'Lord' or 'Jesus', or 'Ma-ra-na-tha' (Come Lord), or whatever else you may prefer, will also help to find that deep still centre within (see the section on the spirituality of John Main, page 50). If a peaceful mind continues to elude you it may be necessary to start again.

Breathing meditations are simple and, as they are not obvious to others, are suitable for your place of work or at spare moments elsewhere. It is important to realise that a breathing meditation without God only creates a peaceful condition that is psychological. If it does not include turning to God, it is neither prayer nor worship. Some people, for physiological reasons, find that such breathing exercises have a negative effect on their search for stillness and they should therefore not persist with them.

These simple preparations are the start of worship. As you turn inwards you could engage in the imaginative worship taught by Ignatius, reading a short story about Jesus or one of his parables and imagine yourself in that situation; or you could reflect on examples of the presence of God in the beauty of creation. Alternatively you could read a short paragraph from the Bible or some other devotional writing. This is best read slowly, seeking the peace in the writing and recognising when it resonates within. Some people find it helpful to prepare a short list of prayers or psalms created from personal preferences, as a fund of devotional matter to draw on. We all have our favourites and the list may be quite short; if you create it yourself it will reflect your unique spirituality, unlike a book prepared by others. The value of such preparation is obvious and is enhanced if you can remember the words instead of having to read them.

There may be a time when the words of the prayer, psalm or reading, or your own thoughts, seem to become 'noisy' and intrusive. If that occurs, cease rehearsing them, let the mind be silent and allow the worship to deepen for you have arrived at that point where you are aware of the peace of God.

DISTRACTIONS

As the mind is no longer full of everyday matters, we now start our period of worship with good intentions, only to find that after a few moments we are thinking about something else. Thoughts arise taking our attention away from God. Instead of achieving a clear focus on God, we may find ourselves thinking rather than worshipping.

I remember a story of a friar walking along a country road being slowly overtaken by a devout nobleman on a horse. They fell into conversation and the nobleman commented on his inability to pray without being interrupted by passing thoughts.

The friar, being a 'professional', said that this was no problem. So the nobleman offered the friar the fine saddle on his horse if he could pray without being distracted by other thoughts. The friar started but after a few minutes he thought "What good is a saddle to me if I do not have a horse?"

It is quite normal for our minds to be busy all day monitoring and assessing the world, making decisions, communicating, reflecting, reliving the past and speculating about the future. Therefore, it is not surprising that our attention can be carried away by our active minds.

A person's attention span is somewhere between five and ten minutes, which means it is difficult for many people to focus on God without interruption for longer than that; as we get older, the attention span becomes shorter and it is harder to hold the awareness of the present moment. The first thing is to recognise that passing thoughts are always there and are part of our human condition. That means they will interfere with our worship and we require some strategies to handle them. One strategy is to recognise each distracting thought, but in general terms only, and without going into its details; following the thought into the everyday gives it energy and will take you away from worship. Then, as it is unnecessary for the moment, gently lay the intrusion aside by ignoring it. Now is the time for worship, so dwell on it no more. This is like being aware of a fly or a wasp buzzing around the room but not following it with your eyes, just letting it be.

If your thoughts are particularly difficult to still, the repetition of a psalm or a prayer may help to focus the mind. This is done as often as is necessary until the whole prayer or psalm has been said without interrupting thoughts. If you realise that you are repeating the words but thinking about something else, then it is best to start again from the beginning and repeat the process. You could use Psalm 23, or 121 or the first part of 139, the Lord's Prayer or some other devotional work. You need not feel restricted to these suggestions, but the shorter the prayer the better. Be aware of any feelings as you turn towards God. With practice this can be reduced to a single line from the psalm or prayer. After a time you can reduce the words to only one or two which remind you of the meaning of the whole of it: this is important, otherwise it has the effect of turning your attention to words instead of turning to God. Replacing unwanted thoughts with one or two significant words with a devotional content is an excellent way of replacing distractions and going deeper into worship. With time and practice it will become easier to slip into stillness.

As you gently let go of the internal 'sounds' of the words, their meaning, rather than their form, fills your awareness. The meaning then becomes so much part of you that it fills your consciousness and you let go of words. As you move deeper into worship the meaning is there in you with every breath you take. It has become so much part of you that just as the prayer is in you, so you are in the prayer, unable to separate yourself from the meaning: so in effect you become the prayer.

In this process, the repetition of the words has not only extended our attention span on God by clearing our minds from discursive thoughts, but has also helped us to orientate ourselves towards God. The conscious part of the mind that creates the distractions is now filled with spiritual thoughts and attitudes, and it gives guidance to that part of the mind of which we are not conscious. In this way we empty the mind of the daily busyness but keep a focus on God, and wait with expectation and anticipation for him to enter the space we have cleared. The clearer the space, the greater is the opportunity for the Spirit. If you are unsure about the notion of emptying ourselves of our busyness during a period of worship, consider for a moment: it is the emptiness of a cup that makes it useful, by enabling it to receive and hold something; similarly, it is the empty space inside a house that enables it to be lived in. So clearing the mind of our daily business enables God to enter and fill it.

Persistent distractions urging you to some action can best be handled by making a very brief note and, if necessary, dealing with the matter later. It may be that over a number of weeks you can discern a pattern to some of the distraction. This not only increases your self-knowledge but may also help to deal with internal or external issues that are not always apparent in other ways.

The importance of self-knowledge now becomes apparent. Reminders of past behaviour may make us feel uncomfortable and disturb our inner stillness as we recognise that our motives were not always as pure as we had believed. We may for example recognise that some of our attitudes are constructed from, or supported by, prejudices. We have to acknowledge and accept that both positive and negative aspects, past and present, are part of us. It is good if we can accept the positive ones without them stimulating our vanity, and come to terms with the negative ones without denigrating ourselves. Being familiar with who and what we are means these thoughts are not so disturbing and enable us to worship more peacefully.

Sometimes, there are so many distracting thoughts that we

seem to make no progress. However the act of gently laying aside each unwelcome thought is also part of worship as our attention, no matter how brief, has been on God. Half an hour spent in this way is time well spent. There is no need to be anxious if the time set aside for worship has been used in this way; it will still have been a positive activity. Dom John Chapman in his *Spiritual letters* suggests that instead of worrying or fighting the problem of distractions, we might laugh at our anxieties instead and in time they will weaken and become easier to handle.

Like many things, these suggestions sound deceptively simple but they require practice. Change will come naturally, if slowly. Dealing with distractions requires patience and time and is not something new. The Desert Fathers and Mothers[7] eighteen hundred years ago had to cope with this difficulty, as did the author of *The cloud of unknowing* in the fourteenth century, and later Brother Lawrence.

In our wish to be close to God, as in any relationship, we are limited in what can be achieved, as the closeness depends on both participants. We do all we can to prepare ourselves, but then we must wait if we want the relationship to develop further because the more we struggle to be close to God the further away he seems to become. Therefore instead of asserting the ego by reciting our needs, insisting on a closeness and expecting an immediate response, we have to lay our wishes and desires aside and simply wait. As we wait, the remnants of the ego are released and we change slowly, almost imperceptibly. Without this reduction and eventual loss of the ego, we will not come closer to God because it is our desires that dominate our thinking and create a barrier. Just as a seed must die in order to produce a beautiful flower, so the ego must die if we hope to be aware of God.

In contemplative worship we seek God, leaving the awareness of our body, the world and even our identity behind. This way of worship is principally a longing of the heart with preparation by the intellect.

Having started worship it is helpful to be aware of how we feel at that moment: whether we are relaxed, at peace, irritated, angry, and so on. Feelings do affect our worship, so to recognise where they come from will help us to understand them, and it makes them easier to accept. Negative feelings are not to be despised, nor rehearsed in any way, but simply acknowledged and humbly offered to God.

The occasions when we should not push our thoughts and feelings aside are when we have difficulties in our lives that require attention. If we are confused and stressed, we should bring our pain or restlessness to God, leave the matter with him and then simply rest in his Light (see "Experiment with Light", page 36). While the difficulties will not disappear, their burden has been shared. We can only be who we are: to pretend otherwise is self-deceiving and is an attempt to deceive God. To reduce the potency of any negative feelings and the situations that created them, do not recall any detail as you will then only relive the past and make your condition worse.

If you are finding silent worship a bit of a struggle, then try the following as a start into silent worship. It should not be followed slavishly and may be modified to suit the individual. Try each step only for as long as it feels comfortable, initially for a minute or so; later it can be for longer.

- Sit in silence for a minute or two: slow down, remain still, just sit, let thoughts come and go.

- After a short time, listen to the silence.
- Then be aware of the present – the seat, the surroundings, your feelings, the silence.
- Sense the inner stillness.
- Do not struggle to do what you think you should be doing; wait, be patient.
- As the active mind slows down, the 'noise' of thoughts will stop. The silence becomes peaceful as you turn towards God with a very short prayer, extract from a psalm or other reading, seeking the company of the Spirit.
- Just rest and be still.

A BUSY LIFE

Finding time for worship, reflection or meditation is never easy and the minute-by-minute pressure of a busy career in industry has made me appreciate just how precious time and opportunity are and how important it is to make the best use of them. Added to the demands of the workplace are the demands of family life such as cleaning, cooking and shopping, not forgetting the importance of setting aside time to nurture relationships with children and partners. If a partner or a spouse is unsympathetic to your form of worship, it may be difficult to find time and a quiet place. Those with a young family have the added difficulty of waiting until the children are asleep before they are able to find a time for worship. Retirement does not necessarily bring greater opportunities: many people who are retired from regular employment find that they are even busier since leaving work. If we were free of the cares of daily life – going to work, paying bills, shopping – then there would be plenty of opportunities to set times aside for worship, but in reality we cannot just cut ourselves off from the world.

We may well seek or respond to that of God in others during our daily contacts, and attend communal worship regularly, but struggle to find time for our daily periods of private worship. It is therefore necessary to have strategies in place which will enable us to use occasional moments as and when they present themselves. These preparations will be slightly different to the leisurely occasions for worship at home. The situations described here may not all be encountered by everyone.

TIME AND PLACE

Amid the hustle and bustle of our activities we need to give ourselves time to return to our 'inner room'. For any styles of worship, not just the silent variety, any odd moment no matter how brief can be an opportunity to retreat, but finding those brief moments can be problematical in mentally demanding situations or when we are engrossed in our activities. However, some simple spiritual activities enable turning inwards easier and with practice this can then become second nature. They can be as helpful in a noisy or busy environment as in the peace of a retreat house. It is necessary to retreat from preoccupations, and to cease talking in our heads. In this receptive frame of mind we turn our attention towards God and wait for him in silent passive receptivity. Gradually we will be led into a deeper level.

You can withdraw to your quiet interior for a few moments while on the train, the bus or simply waiting in a queue; even the waiting room at the doctor or the dentist can be opportunities for a few moments of worship. If silent worship is attempted on public transport you do have the benefit of arriving at your destination in a more peaceful frame of mind, although it is sometimes difficult to ignore distractions and achieve a deep stillness on a crowded bus or train.

If you have to respond to callers or customers, or you are in an executive position, opportunities may be rare and you will need to recognise them when they arise. If this is difficult then instead of *waiting* for opportunities it becomes necessary to *create* them. One way is to use a quiet alarm that can produce a gentle tone to act as a reminder. A similar strategy can help while immersed in worship on public transport, or with a schedule to work to. Relying on a simple discreet reminder gives us the assurance that you do not miss your appointment or your destination.

You can use the method of repeating a significant word with each breath, or repeating a prayer or psalm until you are at peace or the time runs out. You may only have time to say a single word or phrase once only, but this may be sufficient to help to focus your mind on God. Such reminders then co-exist in an unobtrusive way with the vigilance of your journey. It is also helpful to make some simple preparations before you have to cope with these pressures, with a list of prayers, psalms or readings as suggested in "Daily activities" (page 84).

Other opportunities are in places where you can have a certain amount of solitude and freedom from intrusions. If it is not possible to find a time at home then it is worth considering the use of the car in the car park at the start of the working day, and again during lunchtime; or a similar location can be used when shopping. Alternatively you may find a local church or library where it may be possible to sit quietly at lunch time. Ideally, look for a place where interruptions by people, phones, traffic or other noises are minimal.

Do not be anxious if there are only a few minutes available when a much longer time for worship had been hoped for, for even this short period is part of eternity. Instead of dismissing odd minutes as not being worthwhile, acknowledge that this is the best you can hope for at this time. Accept this, and the fact that everything other than this present moment is beyond your control, and then you can begin to relax and savour the peace that is brought by the Spirit. If sustained periods of worship are not possible, do not be anxious as even a fleeting attention to God is worthwhile.

PRESSURE

Achieving a measure of stillness when there is pressure and the adrenaline is flowing is difficult and often impossible. Even in these conditions, a momentary turning to God is worthwhile even though it appears to be futile. Offering a situation to God even if the clamour does not go away means you have a fleeting moment in which to recall the other dimension of your life. If there is insufficient time or the conditions are too difficult, do not despair, stop and try again later, since struggling to create the desired conditions can only result in tension.

Sometimes it is tempting to try to do all your tasks quickly in order to free up a little time for turning to God. However, rushing around can take on a momentum of its own until when you stop you are unable to catch your breath, let alone find a stillness for worship. It is better to turn your attention towards God while working, and then gently do the task so that it becomes an integral part of your worship (see "Practical matters", page 84).

There are times when recalling an earlier peaceful and still occasion can be helpful. If your spiritual life is full, then you do not feel pressures in quite the same way.

Another way of coping with pressure is to focus on completing tasks one at a time and with deliberation ignore the distracting clamour of the others. So for example, if you are walking towards a door you should not anticipate what has to be done when you arrive at the other side; do not hurry but walk slowly and gently, thinking only about the movement of every step as if you are treading on delicate flowers. This is practising the awareness of the present moment.

The pressure of extra commitments and responsibilities, which many people have to cope with in their work, can be very demanding especially when faced with unreasonable or difficult customers or colleagues. We need to quietly resist circumstances which are pushing us away from God, as acceding to this pressure will destroy any internal peace, leaving us tense unable to settle down; but if it becomes impossible to withstand it is best to try to accept the situation in good humour, and acknowledge there is little we can do about it. This is better than taking our resistance so far that we will be 'burnt at the stake' for our beliefs and practices and possibly lose our job. That is neither detachment nor humility. Sometimes, no matter how much we have attempted to develop an interior stillness, we can be tried too much so that frustration and anger arises. It is necessary to recognise that these negative reactions arise from within, and then consider how to manage them in the future. Pressure from abuse, physical or mental bullying is outside the scope of this book, but they should not be tolerated and help should be sought as soon as possible.

The demands made upon us by today's world are considerable and if left unchecked may disrupt our lives to such an extent that it seems as if we are no longer in control of our lives, and opportunities for worship may be passed over in order to respond to demands from others. Modern communications including e-mails and mobile phones are an integral part of daily life and may demand not only an instant response, no matter what else we are doing, but can also be very time consuming and create pressure. The mobile phone in particular has changed the way we live our lives and communicate. Some people seem to expect us to be always available whether we are at home, at work or at leisure; even on holiday we are expected to respond to the demands of work. Unless attempts to satisfy these demands are handled in a controlled way, we will lose our ability to be still and find time to turn to God. We may well have a vocation to be at the service of others, but if that is not balanced with time for ourselves then life can become very one-sided.

There are no easy answers to the difficulty of finding time to cater for the needs of others while at the same time having enough space to address your own needs. The starting point could be to switch off the mobile phone for a few moments or put it on 'silent', and use the resulting space in time to slow down and taking the opportunity to turn to God. Ultimately however, you have to decide what it is that you want from life and then ask yourself whether you want a lifestyle that brings such pressures. People who have family or dependants may be left with little choice but to accept the pressure, whether from work or social commitments. It will take time, months perhaps – even years to become proficient in coping with difficulties, but if you continue your efforts, then settling down for a period of worship will become easier and more rewarding.

If you can reduce the pressures from others there will always be something else demanding your attention, be it preparing a meal, washing dishes or cleaning the floor. Your activities can be part of the worship period, and in that way you 'bring' your activities to God and do all your activities *with* God. The important thing is to slow down and focus on God and to be aware that whatever you do, you do it *with* God and then it is no longer, "*I* am doing something" but "*we* are doing something".

Travelling can be hectic and stressful particularly if you are short of time for a train or a flight. Whenever possible, it is worthwhile trying to find a few moments to offer the journey and your feelings to God so that, in a sense, he becomes like a travelling companion and your calmness and peace are recovered and maintained.

Another effective way of including God in our daily lives involves briefly seeking the guidance of the Spirit before interacting with others, say during a conversation or in discussion. In all these ways worship becomes central to our lives. This approach is easier to accomplish when we are doing simple physical rather than mental activities but it is necessary to remember to do this regularly. As we become more practised seeking a sense of the divine presence, the desire to *strive* to do something *with* God slowly diminishes and eventually ceases. We no longer have to imagine him to be with us because now have a non-intrusive awareness of God and are no longer without the sense of his presence.

Interlude 2
My childhood journey

As my father was in the Luftwaffe and usually away from home, my parents thought it would be safer if we moved eastwards away from Berlin to Lower Silesia, now in Poland. There we lived in a little farmhouse, well away from towns that might be targets for bombing, and began to enjoy the peace and tranquillity of the countryside. The peace however was not to last, since the effects of the aspirations of the Third Reich were never far away. In their drive for absolute power, the Nazi Party's imperative for control was putting pressure on the churches. It was at this point my parents realised that the time was long overdue for my brother (aged three) and me (aged six) to be baptised. My mother approached the local Lutheran pastor who baptised us in secret at the farmhouse with our grandparents becoming also our godparents.

After two summers, idyllic for an adventurous young boy, the winter of 1944/45 came upon us and, much to the fear of all in our village, so too did the advancing Russian army. Once it became obvious the Russian advance could not be halted, there was no alternative but to pack a few essentials and prepare to leave immediately. Once again we were on the move but this time on foot westwards. The start was not very promising; the woods behind us were on fire and we thought we were doomed to die in the crossfire of the Russians and the retreating German army. However, as if by a miracle, there appeared from behind the Russian lines an empty open-topped goods train. Seizing the opportunity to escape, the whole village, harbouring mixed feelings of relief and panic and not considering what might lie ahead other than the promise of safety, scrambled into the open wagons. We ignored the frost and falling snow and were simply relieved to be moving westward out of immediate danger. We travelled in the open wagons for a number of days feeling cold, wet and weary and longing for warmth and security. We eventually commandeered an empty passenger train and arrived late one night in a large town.

No sooner had we arrived than the city lights went out, the air raid sirens sounded and the bombing started. It was 13 February 1945, and that town was Dresden. The incendiary bombs burnt not only the whole city but also burned alive between 33,000 and 100,000 people (estimates vary) in one of the worst events of the war. With an amazing presence of mind the train driver reversed our train, packed with refugees, out of town in the direction from which we had come. Slowly and with immense relief we inched our way out of Dresden and watched from a distance as the whole city burned like a gigantic inferno. The memory of the event still haunts me. Perhaps *this* was the occasion when I learnt the prayer "Lieber Gott, mach mich fromm . . . ." It was certainly a time when we all prayed. The following day another wave of bombing came over what remained of the city, but by that time our train had been re-routed and we were obliged to vacate it soon after. The subsequent trek to the west on foot was long and arduous and much of what happened is as vivid to me today as it was 67 years ago. Tired legs, sleepless nights in cold barns and gnawing hunger were part of our daily routine.

I will never forget the suffering of my fellow refugees,

many of who had inadequate clothing and footwear and no possessions other than the clothes they wore. I am still deeply affected by the memory of an old man, dressed in his Sunday best, struggling to push his elderly infirm mother to safety in a wheelbarrow. He was tired and desperate and begged my brother and me, aged four and seven respectively, to help him. There was also the hunger of the non-German prisoners of war; without cans for food they desperately sought any bit of rubbish which might hold a ladle full of soup. This experience was compounded in my young mind by stories from my father, on his return from the battle of Stalingrad, when he described how Russian prisoners of war were so hungry that they resorted to eating their dead comrades – a fearful image for a seven year old. As refugees we were more fortunate than the prisoners because we could beg for food. Going from door to door we learnt that a large farm could provide shelter in the barn and perhaps some bread, but there were also occasions when farmers who had had too many refugees would set their dogs on us. Those families who had little to give gave what they could, even if it was only a bowl of soup made from hot water and a spoonful of flour. I disliked begging for food, and where possible left my mother and brother to do it. This meant that I would sometimes have to wait alone for hours in the evening twilight guarding our hand-cart until they returned. After all those years, when I now see a person begging my memory is stirred and my heart goes out to them, wondering what misfortune brought them to this point.

The year was 1945. Spring and early summer were on their way bringing warmer weather and with it some hope of better days ahead, but unfortunately we were only hours ahead of the advancing Russian army. I remember one day in particular as we trekked along a straight dusty road with a hot sun beating down. On our right were the remnants of a strafed and burnt-out military convoy, brown with rust and with so many holes that it looked like a grotesque sieve or a three-dimensional war memorial. The only sound in the deserted countryside was the engine of a plane circling overhead. We realised its unfriendly nature as it started its descent, heading straight for us. We dropped everything and ran as far as we could from the centre of the road leaving exposed our few belongings in the handcart. Our mother pushed us to the ground and lay on top of us in the expectation that her body would stop any bullets. Luckily the plane flew on with no one injured but from then on we became very wary whenever we heard or saw an aeroplane. I well remember the anger and frustration of my mother when on similar occasions I would run in terror in the opposite direction to her and bury my face in the grass. After such occasions I would be at the receiving end of her anger, fuelled by fear and relief.

Only a few events have been recorded here but there were many others. Sixty years later as I looked at her frail body lying on her deathbed, it was difficult to imagine the strength of character of the woman, my mother, who was willing to make such sacrifices to bring her two sons to safety. I have much love for her and admire all that she endured to overcome those trying times.

In 1949 my mother returned to England with my brother and me to start a new life. While our arrival in England provided us with food, shelter and security, it was made difficult by some anti-German feelings that were still prevalent. In order to overcome some of these difficulties it became necessary not only to change our surname but also to play down our German background, particularly at school. This meant denying our past: our language, songs, happy memories and customs, such as the German Christmas, in order to have an easier life.

Little stirred in my religious consciousness until the time when, at the age of twelve years, I was disappointed that a prayer to Jesus did not result in the disappearance of the noises in a creaking house, noises that I thought were ghosts trying to catch me.

Our arrival into a stable community in England also enabled me to have a settled time for education. In the first few years after the war, the German schools that were still standing had been used to accommodate the troops of the occupying forces, which meant that learning to read and write was impossible. When I was in the presence of my friends at the Quaker youth club in England my lack of education became apparent to me. The feeling of inequality with my peers, who all attended grammar schools, drove me in search of ways to extend my education generally and in particular in engineering as well as in my spiritual life. At the age of fifteen, I was struggling with what to believe and how to behave. There was so much in the Gospels and even more in the letters to young churches that it became very bewildering.

One Sunday morning I decided to start from scratch, abandon all, and only accept what resonated within. In a logical manner I decided also to discard even the notion of the existence of God. During the following two weeks I became so uncomfortable with the loss of God that it became necessary to accept his existence and that became the starting point of the next stage of my spiritual journey. From then on, the priority was and still is my relationship with God. Everything else flows from that, my beliefs, my attitudes and decisions; considering whether to accept the virgin birth; campaigning for nuclear disarmament; or removing an earthworm from the pavement to the grass where it would have a better opportunity for continuing its life. I was in a partnership with God doing what was required. I became aware of 'that of God' in others and through their words and deeds I saw something of God.

The fears from my wartime childhood are still with me. Recently I found myself hiding behind a tree watching with relief at what was only a police helicopter receding into the distance, but if I am caught unawares the fear of an aircraft is as real today as it was sixty years ago. Occasionally an unexpected reminder in the media, a smell or a sound recalls some of the ghosts of the past, and while they cavort and play in my mind, my life is on hold. At times I am obliged to compare these occasions with the stillness of silent worship in which there is no past, no future and no fear, only a deep peace in which the presence of God is mediated through a feeling of love so intense that sometimes it borders on the ecstatic. For such times I prefer to use the German term *Die Stille*, which for me is not just silence but a place of tranquillity where impressions of love and peace are woven finely into the fabric of the present.

The absence of God

Even when we have experienced closeness to God, there may be times when the love that has been surrounding us no longer seems to exist, and we begin to think that God has deserted us. Eventually we may even consider the possibility that perhaps God was simply a creation of our imagination. Not everyone has such an experience, but it can affect both those whose worship is vocal and those whose worship is contemplative. These feelings of loss and loneliness are intense and can have various causes.

Simply trying too hard to reach out to God by praying for long periods can bring about spiritual fatigue; and if you are following the apophatic way (see page 79) remember to ensure that when considering a negative proposition, a positive one always accompanies it. But it also occurs when difficulties in our lives have caused us such pain that we have withdrawn into ourselves, and this has dulled our sensitivity to and awareness of God's presence. When the stress from problems is light, recovery can be relatively quick, but if we have been affected by traumatic events or been exposed repeatedly to impossible conditions then we may feel so raw and hurt that we doubt the very existence of God. In such circumstances a longer time of healing is necessary before we are able to recognise that God is still with us and is only absent in our perception. Our perception of God can also be affected while taking mood-controlling medicines, and at such times all we can do is accept the situation humbly and continue to worship in our community as best we can until our condition improves.

In extreme cases, the loss of the love of God can be so penetrating and overpowering that we are left feeling bereft and empty, convinced that God has rejected us, resulting in a discomfort of the first degree and leaving an empty space in our lives with no present, no future and, more painfully, no God. We may be reminded of periods of spiritual dryness experienced in the past, but this is deeper, more desolate, and more uncomfortable, with the loss of love and joy that we learnt in earlier days were the movement of the Spirit. There is a continuing lack of enthusiasm and interest in communal worship; loss of interest in private prayer, with an inability to reflect or meditate; no interest in devotional reading, and a loss of proactive spiritual behaviour. The spiritual trauma is impossible for others to imagine; it is cold and empty and presents a landscape of our spiritual journey that is bleak and desolate. We may be reluctant to share these feelings and doubts with others in case we are misunderstood or considered peculiar, and so we are likely to withdraw into silent loneliness, but that compounds the agony.

If this happens, you may wonder what has occurred to change the relationship, because from your perspective it has been good: you have been faithful in your worship and 'attendance' on God, and can find no reason why this change has come about. You have been friends with God, but now it all appears to have changed: you may conclude that this is none of your doing and, without realising it, you would be right.

The explanation of this condition is straightforward if a little unexpected. When we embarked on our contemplative journey a number of things changed. Apart from simplifying our life-style and seeking interior stillness, we strove for humility and detachment, which led us towards waiting on God without our wishes and desires intruding. We have emptied ourselves of proactive worship without replacing it with something else. By ending verbal prayer and starting to listen to God, we also ceased demanding his attention. Until then, our private worship had been based on *our* wishes, *our* desires and on *our* terms, that is, when *we* were ready for prayer. Our worship is now no longer controlled by the ego and we are seeking to be with God on his terms, not our terms.

These significant changes took place so slowly that we did not notice them. It is rather like admiring the wonders of a sunset with its beautiful colours, shapes and light. One minute we are completely absorbed in the glory that lies before us and the next, without being aware of the very gradual changes that are taking place in the sky, we are in darkness with little more than a memory and a sense of loss. Likewise, the changes in our spiritual life have been so gradual that they too have gone unnoticed. It is not the change in our worship that has altered the relationship with God, but rather the reverse. The relation-ship has changed the nature of our worship and consequently the new, developing relationship requires another approach.

Those who have survived such isolation and uncertainty have discovered that this is not a cul-de-sac in their spiritual journey but rather a new start in their relationship with God. This is not the time to struggle and pray harder, since striving and impatience will not improve this situation. This new phase is quite different from what has been experienced previously. In this difficult period, when there is nothing, we need to be gentle with ourselves. To become anxious, or force ourselves into a frenzy of devotional activities similar to earlier times, would be counter-productive and only set the relationship back. God is not 'out there' miles away, nor has he ceased to exist, even though it may feel like that. He is still with us, in fact very close: it is only our awareness of him that has changed. Normally the closer we are to something the clearer it becomes, but this is not so with God; we find that the closer we become, the less we recognise him. The very closeness to God has resulted in this 'nothingness' which is also sometimes referred to as 'darkness', a word that stems from our inability to recognise God. Moses experienced this darkness when he met God in a cloud (Exodus 19:9, 20:21, 24:15–18), and John of the Cross refers to it as the 'night of the soul'. The author of *The cloud of unknowing* experienced this and encouraged the reader to be 'at home' in this condition rather than struggling to leave it, for while we are in this darkness we are close to God. What we must do is acknowledge the existence of the darkness and realise that it is impossible to dispel it, because we are not able to comprehend him with any of our human senses.

When we have reached this new stage in our journey, the old ways of worship that were good and helpful in the past are no longer adequate and are being replaced with a new way of being with God that has to be viewed from a new perspective. The desolation that we perceive is a door that can only be opened by God, but we must first remove as much as we can of our unhelpful attitudes that create a barrier. It is not possible to do anything other than continue in this state of spiritual agony and accept our condition as we would a cold: it is not pleasant, but we just carry on. While we continue to long for him the initiative comes from him, and all we can do is wait; wait with our face turned towards him in hope, expectation, love and with patience; wait on the Spirit.

Waiting with passive longing in the middle of such discomfort is difficult, but it is the start of a different direction on the spiritual journey. Waiting is not easy at the best of times, and when there appears to be no progress and little hope of any change it is even more difficult. Waiting for a bus may last ten minutes or an hour, but waiting for the Spirit can take months, perhaps even years, and can be one of the most difficult stages in the spiritual journey. It is a time when all our qualities of patience, detachment, and equanimity are tested to the limit. It is a time when we have to remind ourselves that God is still close and has not deserted us. At such times the foundation of our faith, reinforced by our religious community with its regular worship and activities, is the only thing that can give us the hope and strength to persevere. We may experience doubt and loss but should not abandon our beliefs or the religious teachings we have received, because they have played their part in bringing us to this point. However, as we continue our journey we may find that some parts become less important than others. This whole period is not an intellectual process but is experiential, and of the heart.

If you are in this state of darkness it may help to talk to someone who has had a similar experience, but it is necessary to be aware that when they share an account of their own spiritual journey it will be different to yours, and may not be entirely helpful. There may even be those who take on the role of 'Job's comforters' and give much unhelpful advice. Talking to someone who has had training in spiritual direction can be helpful, but if you are unable to identify such a person then ask a person with whom you can share spiritual matters – a 'soul friend' or 'spiritual friend' – to listen. In a Quaker meeting the elders have a responsibility to find spiritual support of this kind. Living through this condition and surviving without support is possible but not easy, and there is the risk of losing your way in strange notions that ultimately do not lead to God.

Gradually, despite the doubts and discomfort, a steadfast conviction develops that we are on the right path and not at the end of the road. That we are going in the right direction becomes a certainty and it is necessary to hold onto this as it will keep us going when everything else seems negative. Gradually we start to experience unexpected moments of involuntary stillness and peace. Something is there which was not there before, rather like the dew that appears imperceptibly out of the emptiness of the night. It arrives so gently we are unaware of its approach, yet in the empty, barren cold grey light of the early dawn, it is there. We have been changed. Something has changed us and we feel closer to the whole of creation and to God – the God we know but do not know . . . the God who just is. This certainty is accompanied by a feeling of freedom and a steadfast love for all humanity. There is no desire to return to earlier stages of our spiritual journey because we have begun a new stage that will be quieter and less variable in spiritual terms, but more persistent and reassuring. There is a confidence, and a peace that fills the whole being. The 'valley in the shadow of death' has been traversed and left behind, and a new phase of our journey has started.

Worship: Moving deeper

As we move deeper into worship we cease verbalising; all thinking is left behind as we wait in peace for God with passive receptivity. Instead of striving to tell God of our concerns by frequent prayers, and so monopolising the communication with devout chatter, we give him our undivided attention and listen. With our attention focused exclusively on God, this is a time to wait in silence "with a loving gaze" (Brother Lawrence; *Practising the presence,* p. 35), recognising that this is a completely separate facet of life. It is a focus without discursive thought and directed onto something that cannot be understood. Our focus on God has hope and expectation but is without specific qualities or outward confirmation and without an image. If we do have an image that is helpful we should not prematurely reject it; it will go when the time is right. In this time of waiting we are so focused that although the mind is fully alert the senses are not aware of the body or its surroundings.

We have changed the nature of our worship, so rather than actively seeking God, we recognise only a longing, a purpose, and a hope. Seeking that closeness then becomes our long-term aim rather than the immediate target; there is no urgency in getting there, only a feeling of what may eventually be possible. Indeed the aim is no longer in the front of our thinking but in the background of our minds, so that we are hardly aware of its existence. We are waiting to be *drawn* by what we seek instead of being *driven* by our desires.[8] This is about letting go until nothing is left in us except our longing; it is not a weakening of our devotions but a change taking place in our worship. Anthony Bloom gives examples of this attitude. A worshipper sought his advice, having prayed the Jesus Prayer almost continually for fourteen years and never perceived God's presence. His reply was:

> light a lamp before your Icon […] look around the room where you have been praying […] it is a long time since you have seen your room, then take your knitting and for fifteen minutes knit before the face of God, but I forbid you to say one word of prayer. […] Just knit and try to enjoy the peace. (*School for prayer*, p. 60)

This was to be a time of waiting on God without thought. Bloom also gives the story of a French peasant who used to sit for hours in the chapel motionless and apparently doing nothing. When the priest questioned him about his apparent inactivity, he replied, "I look at him, he looks at me, and we are both happy" (p. 62).

We are now developing an internal silence into which we can retreat. Outward silence is physical, but here is a deep inner silence. This is not just an absence of thoughts but a peaceful inner stillness with a positive quality that we can almost feel. It is an internal condition where in the stillness of the mind we are separated from the everyday busyness of our lives. As the clamour of our incessant thoughts subsides, we find a deep peace. There is no striving. Here we just 'are', no longer occupied with cares and desires, wishes or dreams. Here, time has no power as we are held in timeless space, in a moment of eternity in which love and peace permeate our whole being. This is not just a comfortable feeling but deep inner peace that cannot be adequately described. It is a peace that we know is God. In this emptiness from preoccupation with self we have the freedom to turn to him unhindered.

This is the inner room to which Jesus referred, in which we can turn to God in secret (Matthew 6:6). Here, our whole attention is turned towards him as we remain still, reaching out to him. It is a time when words or a statement of belief is superfluous. This unconditional orientation of our total life towards God is silent worship of the heart, a life grounded in God. It is worship not of a heart that just loves God, but a heart that knows God; the heart that has walked with God and has undertaken activities with a sense of the divine presence. This grows out of the quality of our lives and out of the countless times we have turned to God, when we have either sought him or tried to live with an awareness of him. This is a real dimension of our subjective existence.

As we become aware of God's presence all noise and distracting thoughts recede into the background; we are enveloped in an ever-deepening sense of peace impossible to convey in words. The awareness of our place of worship, the world around us, even the voices of people and everyday noises are no longer heard; we are left with something so profound that there are neither feelings nor an awareness of self. It is not sleep, which entails a loss of consciousness, nor is it a passive wakefulness as the awareness of who and what we are has been suspended. Moments such as these are indescribable yet gentle, peaceful and filled with a deep joy. We are filled with a powerful feeling of love, seeking for nothing other than to remain in this condition. As travellers on our spiritual journey we have arrived home. No longer do we wait in front of a closed door; it is now open. He is with us and we are with him. We are no longer worshipping the God out there; we are now with God, the God who is nowhere but is everywhere… the God who is indescribable… the God who just is. It is total oblivion.

In this intimacy with God, we lose the awareness of all we desire, all that we have and all that we are. The condition belongs to a wholly different sphere of existence in which a new kind of relationship has developed; a condition in which we are no longer preoccupied with our self-interests. Our relationship with him is based on terms that we cannot comprehend; it is without words or any residual longing to be with God as that has been fulfilled. It is no longer a matter of trying to set our self-interests to one side because they are no longer there.

Such an experience is without awareness of time, space, or even existence, as we seem to have been suspended in a moment of eternity. It might only have lasted an instant but there will be surprise when the clock is checked afterwards. The memory too has been suspended so there is no recollection of what took place. We came through the 'cloud of forgetting' where we leave behind memory and thinking, into the 'cloud of unknowing' where we are close to God but are not able to comprehend him; where nothing is of consequence and we seek no understanding. Afterwards we realise that we have been so close to God that we were spiritually intimate in what is described by Meister Eckhart as a place where God and the ground of our soul coincide. Such experiences are powerful, beautiful, and gentle, with feelings of being enveloped by deep love, a condition impossible to describe.

Just as our will, our life and our thoughts enable us to live fully in the physical world, so too does the spiritual side enable us to live in a wholly different world for which words are inadequate. We have lost the awareness of self and are devoid of anxiety. We are curiously relaxed and unhurried as we go about our daily activities with a newly found freedom; we experience a strong love for the world, everything and everybody. There is a feeling of warmth and joy towards all humanity and we feel able to face any difficulty we may encounter.

Our behaviour and our attitude to life have undoubtedly been affected. Silent worship has changed us. It is no longer something we do but something we are. The richness of our spiritual life, made up of the layers of prayer, spiritual habits and practices, culture and our life experiences, as well as the books we have read, have brought us to this point. They have shaped our outlook and our attitude to God and to the world. Imperceptibly we have become what we have read, studied and tried to live and that, in part, determines our relationship with God, but in the end he is the major factor affecting our relationship. We can prepare ourselves and seek an awareness of him as much as we want, but those deep moments only occur when God responds. In the early days of our spiritual lives, an element of our longing may have been to do his will, but now we turn to God in the hope to be with him and live out our lives with the consequences of that experience. The intimacy of the relationship varies with each individual and it can never be predicted or taken for granted. For those whose lives are particularly complicated and busy, such moments may not be frequent.

INVOLUNTARY WORSHIP

There are now occasions in our lives when on brief and unexpected occasions, we are once again held in those peaceful moments. The world around us slows down, as we are held in an unreal moment, in a moment of eternity. If we are busy with a task, or are surrounded by people, we may feel the need to turn inward. A deep and powerful feeling of love transcends everything and envelops us. It feels as though a blanket of love and peace is covering us. Things that have been clamouring for attention just slide off our shoulders and become unimportant. On such occasions it is clear that we are not reaching towards a faraway God or praying *to* him, but rather are *with* him and being held without any effort on our part. There may be other occasions when without warning we are held for an instant when everything around us stands still and is silent. People seem to cease moving while we continue with our simple activities, and even these somehow become unreal. It is a deep and peaceful time. It will pass gently and leave a wonderful joy. Moments such as these come unexpectedly and without warning, leaving us with a feeling of deep peace and an intense love towards all humanity both good and bad. This experience of having been close to God is something to accept with joy but without the expectation of it being repeated.

If we try to hold onto any of these moments, our self-awareness dispels it and it disappears instantly, leaving us with a feeling that something special has happened but we are not sure what. No amount of effort will bring it back. We have no control over such occasions as we cannot control what comes from God. It is easier to grasp the wind or to bring light into a dark room using a bucket full of sunshine.

What next

The next step on your spiritual journey depends on you, the reader. Having read this book you might well decide that such a full commitment is not for you and lay it aside. However, do not throw it away. Not everyone wants to practise this form of worship all the time but you may be moved to try it sometime in the future, and you can use this as a reference book. Or you may have found some parts of the book sufficiently interesting to want to follow them up and see if they work for you. To follow everything can be counter-productive. Nor should you take what has been written here as rules: at best, they are notes that point to a direction. One of John Chapman's favourite maxims was "Pray as you can and do not try to pray as you cannot" (*Spiritual letters* p. 25). What matters in the end is that you do what suits you best. Much depends on your motivation: what is helpful for one person may not be for another, but the way forward is always with God.

Just as life has many phases from childhood through to old age, so too does our spiritual life. Each phase makes its own demands upon our time and energy and provides us with opportunities for developing and growing as a person. We can manage our lives better if we are able to recognise those phases as and when they occur and then give to each what we can.

Any journey brings changes in the scenery and the same is true of a spiritual journey. If contemplative worship is the right way forward for you, it will become obvious but there are some things to bear in mind. To begin with, do not be critical of your past activities since they have brought you to where you are now, even though it may well be that some parts are becoming less important than they used to be. If you engage in communal vocal worship it is advisable to continue with this as well as in silent worship, because one feeds the other. To maintain the ability to find inner tranquillity it is necessary to practice silent worship daily or the ability will leach away. One of the Desert Fathers, Anthony the Great, put it this way:

> Just as fish die if they stay too long out of water, so the monks who loiter outside their cells or pass their time with men of the world lose the intensity of inner peace. Like a fish going towards the sea, we must hurry to reach our cell; for fear that if we delay outside we will lose our interior watchfulness. (*The Sayings of the Desert Fathers*, p. 2)

In addition, some things that are basic to everyone include:

- the necessity to have the appropriate attitudes if we want to develop the relationship with God;
- the necessity to wait on God, as a good relationship with him, like any other, depends on the positive action of both parties;
- the inability to 'know' what God is like in his nature. We can never comprehend God with our senses, and no matter how we describe him, the closer we get to him the less we recognise or understand;
- the need to recognise that God is always present; it is only our awareness that changes. Some people are aware of him only occasionally while others never have that experience.

Whether we are aware of him or not, we cannot escape the ever-presence of God that is so eloquently described in Psalm 139:

> Lord, you have examined me and you know me.
> You know me at rest and in action;
> you discern my thoughts from afar.
> You trace my journeying and my resting-places,
> and are familiar with all the paths I take.
> For there is not a word that I speak but you, Lord,
>   know all about it.
> You keep close guard behind and before me
> and place your hand upon me.
> Knowledge so wonderful is beyond my grasp;
> it is so lofty I cannot reach it.
> Where can I escape from your spirit,
> where flee from your presence?
> If I climb up to heaven, you are there;
> if I make my bed in Sheol[9] you are there.
> If I travel to the limits of the east,
> or dwell at the bounds of the western sea,
> even there your hand will be guiding me,
> your right hand holding me fast.
> If I say, 'surely darkness will steal over me,
> and night will close around me.'
> Darkness is not too dark for you and night is as light
>   as day.
> To you both dark and light are one.

Even though we may have a relationship with God it does not follow that life will be calm, peaceful and unruffled.

However, when we do meet pressures, crises and traumas, we will be able to deal with them in ways that are influenced by that relationship. To strengthen the relationship we need to bring the awareness of God into as many parts of our lives as possible by reducing the power of the ego, thinking more about others and less about us. Rowan Williams writes, in *The wound of knowledge*:

> the practice of selfless attention, self-forgetful attention, to any task is a proper preparation for contemplating God. To be absorbed in the sheer otherness of any created order or beauty is to open the door to God, because it involves that basic displacement of the dominating ego without which there can be no spiritual growth (p. 180).

Whether we are aware of it or not, we are all on a spiritual journey throughout our lives and there will be many opportunities for enrichment and development. We have to be alert to opportunities that point us towards God wherever they may come from, as the Quaker *Advices & queries* ask:

> Are you open to new light, from whatever source it may come? Do you approach new ideas with discernment? (*Advices & queries* 7)

> Remember that Christianity is not a notion but a way (*Advices & queries* 2).

Whenever possible let unresolved spiritual matters or issues of belief lie peacefully, as they may become clearer later, perhaps much later. If questions are not resolved, rather than struggle with them, let them be at rest and they may lose their power as other things become more relevant. As our goal is to be closer to God, it can be helpful if we find someone with whom we can share our journey, a soul friend or a spiritual companion. We have the rest of our lives to live and should aim to live them to the full with God. On occasions the path will be easy but at other times it will be difficult and the way forward seemingly uncertain, perhaps even making us want to turn back. Whatever happens we would do well to be gentle with ourselves and to follow the Psalmist's advice to "Wait quietly for the Lord, be patient till he comes" (Psalm 37:7).

Glossary

The meaning of words and phrases as I understand them.

Abandonment of self – an absolute and total trust in God, having offered all that one has and is, without being prevented by the fear of any negative consequences.

Awareness of God – being aware of an intimate relationship where God is the focus.

Beliefs – the views that we consider to be true.

Centring down – focusing on God during or after the elimination of distractions.

Contemplation – waiting on God with longing and a still, non-discursive mind.

Desire – a wish for something; a want.

Desolation – feeling of being deserted and in misery.

Detachment – the state of not being influenced by emotion, prejudices or desire.

Faith – to accept in faith that the unverifiable religious views being offered are true.

God's will – doing those things that seem right in the context of our relationship with God.

God's response – any spontaneous feelings not controlled by us that remind us of God and which we think or feel may have come from God.

Grace; the grace of God – much can be written about this subject, but the meaning of grace or charism is that it can be a quality or gift from God to a person. The phrase 'The grace of God in a person' refers to a relationship with God that affects and illumines the daily activities of that person; so some people are said to be in a state of grace. 'The grace of God in the world' is about descriptions of unexplained good and beneficent instances assumed to have been initiated by God.

Humility – being humble and non-assertive.

Listening to God – a receptive attitude of mind in which we wait in anticipation.

Meditation – focus on a word, sound, object, image or activity to the exclusion of all else.

Mindfulness – practising the awareness of the present moment (see also Present moment).

Mystical dimension in life – a belief or an experience of reality that surpasses natural or normal understanding or experience.

Offer to God – to hold an issue or a person in the mind while seeking the awareness of God.

Prayer – a reaching out to God with words.

Present moment; being in the present moment – holding in one's consciousness the current activity or condition without engaging in thoughts.

Reflecting – considering the meaning or wisdom of some words or circumstances.

Relationship with God – an ongoing awareness of God and our response.

Sacrament – a rite regarded as a channel for, or a sign of, grace.

Sacramental – an act or object that may transmit or receive grace.

Silent worship – non-vocal worship that can include meditation and contemplation.

Solitude – this is not simply being alone, it is also an internal condition.

Soul friend – a person with whom we can share spiritual matters.

Spiritual life – an ongoing relationship with those things that give direction to our lives.

Spirituality – those internal and external life experiences that give direction to our lives.

Stillness – a state of deep tranquillity.

Worship; contemplative worship – a longing to be with God unaccompanied by words or thoughts.

Endnotes

1. Quaker Peace & Service (QPS) was the department of British Quakers concerned with promoting peace in the world. It is now known as Quaker Peace & Social Witness (QPSW).

2. Later to be known as Quaker Committee on Christian & Interfaith Relations (QCCIR).

3. There are other examples in history of being with God in darkness, e.g. Moses in a cloud on Mount Sinai (Exodus 19:9, 20:21, 24:15–18).

4. In Orthodox spirituality, the heart is not simply the physical organ, but the spiritual centre of the person, the inner sanctum in which the union with God takes place. This union cannot take place solely by efforts of the worshipper as only God can induce it.

5. Metropolitan Anthony Bloom (1914–2003) was head of the Russian Orthodox Church in Great Britain and Ireland (Diocese of Sourozh).

6. I found this phrase in the commentary on the Song of Songs by Gregory of Nyssa (In Cant. XI), quoted in *Light from Light: An anthology of Christian mysticism*, p. 39 (see Bibliography).

7. For *The Sayings of the Desert Fathers*, trans. Benedicta Ward, see Bibliography.

8. This is a bit like 'doing non-doing' in Zen Buddhism; a form of active inactivity.

9. In the Old Testament times, Sheol was the underworld where the spirits of the dead went (2 Samuel 12:23). It was a place of forgetting (Psalm 88:12), a shadowy place where the spirits of the dead continued to exist aimlessly, in misery and without hope. The Psalmist suggests that even here God can find us (see also Psalm 16:10 and 23:4).

Bibliography

These are some of the books that I found helpful and which the reader may want to explore.

GENERAL AND BASIC TEXTS

Chapman, Dom John OSB, *Spiritual letters*, ed. Dom Roger Hudleston, Sheed & Ward, 1946. A valuable book with much good advice on the contemplative method of worship.

The cloud of unknowing, Penguin Classics, 1961. Written c. 1370 by an unidentified person; a devotional classic, it is well worth reading though the theology is of the fourteenth century.

Davies, Oliver, *God within*, Darton, Longman and Todd, 1988. This is a most absorbing account of the mystical traditions of Northern Europe. It includes reviews of Meister Eckhart, Johannes Tauler, Jan van Ruusbroec, Julian of Norwich and others.

A Dictionary of Christian spirituality, and *The Dictionary of Christian theology*, both SCM Press, 1983. Interesting and useful reference books.

Green, Thomas H., *When the well runs dry*, Notre Dame, Ind.: Ave Maria Press, 1979.

Guenther, Margaret, *Holy listening*, Darton, Longman and Todd, 1992. A fascinating presentation of ways of spiritual guidance.

Julian of Norwich, *Revelations of Divine Love*, trans. Elizabeth Spearing, introduction and notes by A.C. Spearing, Penguin Classics, 1998.

Leech, Kenneth, *Soul Friend: Spiritual Direction in the Modern World*, Darton, Longman and Todd, 1994. Primarily about spiritual direction, but an excellent book.

Light from Light: An anthology of Christian mysticism, ed. Louis K. Dupré & James A. Wiseman OSB, Paulist Press, New Jersey, USA, 2001. Extracts of some important writings in Christianity.

The Sayings of the Desert Fathers, trans. Benedicta Ward, Mowbrays, 1975. A classic and a fascinating browse that reveals attitudes of some of the early followers of Jesus.

Lao Tzu, *Tao te ching: An illustrated journey*, trans. Stephen Mitchell, Frances Lincoln, 1999. A very readable translation that has been coloured by the translator's experience of Zen Buddhism.

Thich Naht Hanh, *Peace is every step*, Rider, 1991. A lucid account of the practice of the present moment.

Williams, Rowan, *The wound of knowledge*, Darton, Longman and Todd, 1979. A history of Christian spirituality up to the time of John of the Cross.

WOMEN'S SPIRITUALITY

Belenky, Mary Field & others, *Women's ways of knowing*, Basic Books, 1997.

Celebrating women, ed. Hannah Ward, Jennifer Wild, Janet Morley, SPCK, 1995. An insight into women's spirituality with poetry, prayers and reflections.

Clark-King, Ellen, *Theology by heart*, Epworth Press, 2004. Contains many images of God from a womanly perspective.

Kolbenschlag, Madonna, *Kiss Sleeping Beauty goodbye*, Doubleday, 1979.

Wuellner, Flora Slosson, *Prayer and our bodies*, Upper Room Books, 1997. On womanly spirituality.

AVENUES TO SPIRITUALITY

Quaker:

Many helpful introductory books are available from the Quaker Centre Bookshop, Friends House, 173 Euston Road, London NW1 2BJ.

Gorman, George H., *Introducing Quakers*, Quaker Home Service, 1981. This is now out of print but may be found in Quaker meeting libraries.

Pink Dandelion, Ben, *The liturgies of Quakerism*, Ashgate, 2005.

Quaker faith & practice, The Religious Society of Friends in Britain, 1995. The handbook of the Society reflecting members' current attitudes to life and God.

In the Roman Catholic tradition:

Hughes, Gerard W., *The God of surprises*, Darton, Longman and Todd, 1985. Based on Ignatian spiritual exercises.

Kinn, James W., *Contemplation 2000*, Saint Bede's Publications, Petersham, MA, 1997. A good introduction to John of the Cross.

Brother Lawrence, *Practising the presence of God*, trans. E.M. Blaiklock, Hodder and Stoughton, 1981. A collection of letters and recollections of conversations with Brother Lawrence.

Main, John OSB, *Word into silence*, Darton, Longman and Todd, 1983.

Eastern Orthodox:

Author unknown, *The way of a pilgrim*, and *The pilgrim continues his way*, both trans. R.M. French, SPCK, 1972 and 1973 respectively; also published by Darton, Longman and Todd.

Bloom, Archbishop Anthony, *School for prayer* (Libra Book), Darton, Longman and Todd, 1970. Very readable with practical advice arising from experience.

Dalrymple, William, *From the holy mountain*, HarperCollins, 1998. An account of a journey from Mount Athos through the Orient to Cairo.

Ware, Bishop Kallistos, *The Orthodox way*, Mowbrays, 1979. A general account of the doctrine, worship and life of the Orthodox Church.

Index

Permissions